Images 31 The best of British contemporary illustration 2007

AOI

Images 31

Edited and published by
The Association of Illustrators
2nd Floor, Back Building
150 Curtain Road
London
EC2A 3AT

Tel. +44 (0)20 7613 4328
Fax +44 (0)20 7613 4417
info@theaoi.com
www.theAOI.com

ISBN 978-0-9515448-9-1

Production in China by
Hong Kong Graphics and Printing Ltd
Tel: (852) 2976 0289
Fax: (852) 2976 0292

The Association of Illustrators

AOI Volunteer Council of Management
Beach, Paul Bowman (until February 2007), Russell Cobb, Andrew Coningsby, Adam Graff, Rod Hunt, Simon Pemberton, Robert Swift (until March 2007)

AOI Chair
Russell Cobb

AOI Deputy Chair
Rod Hunt

Company Secretary
Rod Hunt

AOI Images Committee
Silvia Baumgart, Stella Di Meo, Adam Graff, Rod Hunt, Sabine Reimer, William Webb

Advisors
Stephanie Alexander, Alison Branagan, Stuart Briers, Ruth Gladwin, Chris Haughton, Tony Healey, Matt Johnson, Christine Jopling, Robert Lands, Alison Lang, Samantha Lewis, Simon Stern, Fig Taylor, Adrian Valencia, Anna Vernon, Bee Willey, Jo Young

Manager
Silvia Baumgart
silvia@theaoi.com

Marketing and Events Co-ordinator
Stella Di Meo (until April 2007)
events@theaoi.com

Images Co-ordinator
Sabine Reimer
images@theaoi.com

Publications/Membership Co-ordinator
Derek Brazell
derek@theaoi.com

Membership Co-ordinators
Naomi Manning and Nicolette Hamilton
info@theaoi.com

Finance Officer
Ian Veacock BA(Hons) FCCA
finance@theaoi.com

Book Design
Simon Sharville
www.simonsharville.co.uk

Contents

About the **AOI**

The Association of Illustrators was established in 1973 to advance and protect illustrators' rights and is a non-profit making trade association dedicated to its members' professional interests and the promotion of contemporary illustration. As the only body to represent illustrators and campaign for their rights in the UK, the AOI has successfully increased the standing of illustration as a profession and improved the commercial and ethical conditions of employment for illustrators. On behalf of its members and with their continued support, the AOI can achieve goals that it would be difficult or impossible for Creators to attempt alone.

A voice for illustration

The AOI provides a voice for professional illustrators and by weight of numbers and expertise is able to enforce the rights of freelance illustrators at every stage of their careers. The AOI not only enables individual illustrators to deal with today's market, it lobbies parliament to change legislation through the Creators Rights Alliance and the British Copyright Council. AOI liaises with national and international organisations, art buyers, agents and illustrators over industry problems and campaigns against unfair contracts and terms of trade.

Campaigning and Net-working

The AOI is responsible for establishing the right for illustrators to retain ownership of their artwork and helped to establish the secondary rights arm of the Designers and Artists Copyright Society (DACS), the UK visual arts collecting society. In addition, it lobbies parliament for better legislation for illustrators though the Creators Rights Alliance (CRA) and the British Copyright Council (BCC). The AOI is also a founder member of the European Illustrators Forum (EIF) a network of 19 member associations in Europe established to exchange information, co-ordinate exhibitions and conferences and create a stronger force for illustrators within Europe and the European Commission.

Pro-Action: Illustration Campaign and Liaison Group

Pro-Action is a new committee established by the Association of Illustrators and the Society of Artists Agents to deal with the problems facing illustrators in today's market place. Our aims are to tackle fee erosion, increasingly detrimental contract terms from clients and issues that may arise between illustrators and their representatives. These factors have increasingly become a negative force effecting creators of visual material working in the commercial communications arena over the last 25 years.
For further information please visit www.pro-action.org.uk

Information and Support Services

In the past year, the AOI has continued to improve services to its members. Members of the AOI not only sustain campaigning and networking to improve working conditions for all they benefit personally from AOI services.

Members stay informed with our wide range of events and seminars. Varoom magazine, UP info poster and the monthly Despatch newsletter keep members up to date with events, practice and developments in the industry. Members receive up to 50% off our topical range of events and forums, themes ranging from children's books, to self-promotion, business planning and up-to-the-minute industry debates.

Resources to help illustrators succeed

Members receive large discounts on essential publications, including the Images annual, Rights - The Illustrator's Guide to Professional Practice, Survive - The Illustrator's Guide to a Professional Career and our range of targeted directory listings of illustration commissioners. Members of the AOI can receive discounts in art shops around the country.

Resources to help commissioners succeed

The AOI's Guide to Commissioning Illustration will save time and money by guiding commissioners safely through all pitfalls of the commissioning process. Commissioners receive Images the only jury-selected source book in the UK free of charge. Our online portfolios give commissioners looking for the perfect artist for their projects access to more than 8000 classified images and the creator's contact details in a click.

Essential professional and business advice

Members have access to a free dedicated hotline for legal, ethical and pricing advice, discounted consultations with our pool of industry specialists including business advisors, a life coach, chartered accountants and portfolio consultants.

Promotion

Members can receive substantial discounts on the AOI's online portfolios and our Images competition and exhibition, showcasing the best of British contemporary illustration. The annual is the only jury-selected source book, despatched to over 4000 prominent commissioners of illustration in the UK and overseas.

Inspiration

Talks with leading illustrators, industry debates and discounted entry to competitions and exhibitions. Members receive a free subscription to Varoom a 90 page magazine the UK's creative industry has been waiting for. Varoom is a sumptuous celebration of 'made' images. It features interviews with leading illustrators and image-makers as well as in-depth articles on different aspects and themes of contemporary illustration. It's stimulating line-up of interviews, profiles, history and polemic make Varoom essential reading for everyone interested in visual communication.

Contact

To request further information or a membership application form please telephone +44 (0)20 7613 4328

Website

Visit the AOI's website at www.theAOI.com for details of the Association's activities, including samples from current and past Journals, details of forthcoming events and online tickets, the AOI's history, and to order publications and display and show online portfolios

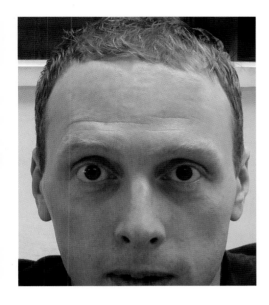

"Digitisation is changing our world, and as with all major change there are rewards as well as dangers."

"The AOI has an invaluable role to play helping illustrators gain from the positives, while acting as an advocate of our members' interests against the negatives of digitisation."

"More than ever we need every illustrator to be a member of this organisation, through subscription, participation, and the visible support of all."

Welcome to the 31st annual edition of Images.

How the AOI is grabbing the reins in a year of change.

In my second year as Chairman of the AOI, one thing has emerged as the overriding trend in illustration: digitisation. We attended events such as the European Illustration Forum in Valencia 2007 and meetings with the BCC (British Copyright Council) and CRA (Creator's Rights Alliance). All were more than a little thought-provoking.

First of all, it's clear that we as illustrators are working in new ways. Websites rather than portfolios have become the window of choice through which clients choose to look at our work. And the media we work in are changing, from physical media like ink and paint to a palette of digital media, or a combination of both. Even the term 'illustrator' itself is beginning to look like an antiquated way to describe the reality of what many of us are now actually producing with the new tools at our disposal.

Less positively, issues are arising which we need to be aware of and find ways to deal with. In our freeware, shareware, free-download generation, the issue of copyright rears its complicated head. The organisations whose councils we sit on are busy dealing with proposed intellectual property legislation as well as organisations intent on the digitisation of publications world wide – all situations which will effect illustrators work, whether on-line or not.

On to other matters.
Our magazine Varoom celebrates its first birthday, reaching an international audience, and with a fanfare of positive reviews in the design press.

I attended the Fumetto Comix festival in Switzerland 2007, and was greeted by the encouraging sight of a lot of exciting self-initiated work, and a British illustration presence.

And Pro-Action, a new committee established by the AOI and the Society of Artists' Agents, has risen to deal with some of the problems faced by illustrators, ranging from fees to rights.

But back to my main theme. Digitisation is changing our world, and as with all major change there are rewards as well as dangers in the new landscape. New tools, along with a fierce competitiveness in the world of illustration, are breeding new approaches, new creativity, and new channels through which we can deliver our talents. As I

mentioned briefly above, illustrators can now move beyond the comfort (or tyranny) of pen and paper into multimedia, animation and 3D. To my mind this is a matter for celebration – it should mean more commissions for more members, more variety in the work we do, and more income for the talented, the versatile and those prepared to embrace this brave new world.

It's an exciting but uncertain time, and the AOI has an invaluable role to play helping illustrators gain from the positives, while acting as an advocate of our members' interests against the negatives. More than ever we need every illustrator to be a member of this organisation, through subscription, participation, and the visible support of all. That means every illustrator in the community - from the aspiring to the household name.

Russell Cobb
AOI Chairman

What is illustration in 2007? Perhaps the only thing we can say with any certainty is that there is no single definition that adequately describes it. Illustration has never been more diverse, more fragmented, more resistant to categorisation. Hardly surprising when we consider that the craft is currently being hammered by cheap photography, by digitally manipulated images, by instant clip art libraries, and by the conviction amongst clients that illustration has too much indeterminacy to be trusted to deliver blunt commercial and editorial messages.

A media landscape without engaging and thought-provoking illustration is like a rural landscape without trees. Bleak. But in critical areas, this is precisely what has happened. Name a popular magazine that uses illustration on its front cover? How many daily newspapers use illustration to do anything other than fill awkward gaps on a page? Book jackets, once the domain of illustrators, are now just as likely to feature photographs (often heavily manipulated). You can add movie posters to the list – it is rare today to find one that is illustrated. In advertising, illustration is an infrequent ingredient. Too risky: too dangerous – or so it seems.

And yet, away from the world of big buck advertising and consumer culture, there are countless instances of illustration's rude health and its protean ability to reinvent itself. We find signs of life in the most unlikely places: computer animation is hugely popular – Pixar is not only owned by Disney, it is the Disney of our era; computer games have surpassed Hollywood in earning power; the graphic novel enjoys intellectual and commercial credibility; one of the most successful pop acts of recent years is Gorillaz – the creation of comic book artist Jamie Hewlett; there are a host of small magazines – Illustrated Ape, Amelia's Magazine – mapping out a subterranean world of drawn imagery; Quentin Blake appears on Desert Island Discs – a feat that propels him to the status of national treasure.

As a graphic designer, I can't help pointing out another aspect of illustration's well-being. Some of the most lauded and feted graphic designers working today are in fact illustrators. They'd never use the 'I' word to describe themselves, but they use hand drawn or computer generated imagery to create free flowing conceptual and abstract work that is undeniably illustrative. I'm thinking of people like the Norwegian designer Kim Hiorthøy, and his compatriots Grandpeople (there are others), whose output constitutes a new hybrid strain of graphic design and illustration. This development is not in the least calculated. It is instinctual and unselfconscious. And there's lots of it around.

The work of Hiorthøy, Grandpeople and others, should not be confused with mainstream graphic design. Most mainstream graphic design is bland and clone-like. We can perhaps admire the business acumen that has led designers – and advertising agencies – to get into bed with brand owners; it is a relationship that has led to designers and advertisers 'owning' the visual landscape – with illustrators feeding off the scraps they leave behind. But it's hard to like or

Introduction by **Adrian Shaughnessy**

Adrian Shaughnessy is a freelance art director and writer. He was co-founder of design group Intro, and its creative director from 1988-2004. During his time at Intro the company won numerous awards and accolades. After 15 years, Adrian left the company to pursue an interest in writing.
He has written and edited three books on radical record sleeve design (the Sampler series), and edited a monograph of Intro work called 'Display Copy Only' (all published by Laurence King). His most recent work is 'How to be a graphic designer without losing your soul'. He writes for all the principal UK design magazines including Eye and Creative Review. Adrian has a monthly column in Design Week, and is a guest contributor to Design Observer, the leading US-based design blog. Since 2006, he is the editor of the Association of Illustrators' new magazine, Varoom – the journal of illustration and made images. He has written about illustration on many occasions. Currently, Shaughnessy is consultant creative director of This is Real Art, a new 'virtual' creative agency which employs a roster of designers, illustrators and film makers. The company works with some of the leading advertising agencies and media companies in the UK and Europe

respect what these brand-centric 'creatives' produce. On the other hand, in an increasingly conformist and homogeneous world, where the slick, retouched image is king, illustration retains the ability to strike a raw note of authenticity and rebellion. It's still the lingua franca of sub-cultural activity. Look at skateboard art; comics; underground music packaging; the Banksy phenomenon; t-shirt culture; the cult of fantasy art – the list goes on. When it wants to be, illustration can be subversive, unsettling and provocative.

This is not to disparage the more gentle forms of illustration that fulfil a purely practical role. The need for everything from instructional diagrams to anatomical studies – even purely decorative effects – is inarguable: just as we need sober and effective graphic design for road signage and bank statements, so we need practical illustration for countless every day functions. What I'm talking about here is the higher calling of illustration, and its inherent capacity to evoke emotion, create aesthetic engagement and transmit ideas.

One of illustration's most distinguishing features is the fact that it is – for the most part – a solo activity. Yes, there are some illustration partnerships and a few collectives, but the vast majority of illustration is done alone, a characteristic it shares with writing. Of course, writers have editors and illustrators have art directors to shape and mould their creative production, but the act of filling a blank page with prose or imagery usually begins as a solitary undertaking.

It's fitting that illustrators and writers should share the same solitary working conditions, because great writing is largely made by the same set of factors that make great illustration: psychological insight; narrative power; stylistic accomplishment; technical adroitness. Illustration shares with writing the ability to make us think. It may lack the written word's ultimate ability to articulate complex argument and to render the abstract comprehensible, but it offers a unique vantage point for speculation and conjecture.

Illustration can be many things: a source of humour, of style, of nostalgia, of surrealist wonder. As a satirical weapon, it can be deadly – think of the great political caricaturists like James Gillray, Gerald Scarfe, Ralph Steadman and David Levine. These men could encapsulate the villainy of our political masters with a few deft lines. As the infamous Boss Tweed, the 19th century American politician and head of Tammany Hall, once said, he didn't care so much what the papers wrote about him because his constituents couldn't read, but dammit, he said, they can see pictures.

The symbiotic relationship between writing and illustration runs deep. There are many writers who are also illustrators: Edward Lear, Maurice Sendak, Mervyn Peake. There also numerous writer and illustrator partnerships: Charles Dickens and George Cruickshank; Lewis Carroll and Sir John Tenniel; AA Milne and EH Shepherd; Neil Gaiman and Dave McKean.

These pairings are inseparable. We can't think of one without thinking of the other. But today we see something new. Increasingly we see illustrators not only writing their own text, but "drawing" their own text – in other words, making the text an integral part of the image. Immediately we think of Paul Davis, David Shrigley, David Hughes, Olivier Kugler, and others. Here are illustrators striving to extend their aesthetic and narrative reach by adding text to their images. Artists like Davis and Shrigley are forging a future for illustration where it is unshackled from its traditional role as a mere "illuminator" of text; with them, the illustration is the text, and vice versa.

But it is illustration's ability to evoke emotion that is its greatest attribute. As the graphic designer Angus Hyland noted recently in his compendium of contemporary illustration The Picture Book, "we first engage with art or picture-making at an early age through children's books. Illustration, rather than what we think of as fine art, forms the basis of our aesthetic education." For most of us, growing up in households with books, Hyland's observation will strike a chord. Epiphanic encounters with the great illustrators of children's literature form a common thread that runs through the life of many people.

My own epiphany – aged 5 – was engendered by a musty copy of Robert Louis Stevenson's A Child's Garden of Verses. This book had watercolours and line drawings by Millicent Sowerby: her paintings were dreamy visions of an idealised life; elegant ladies in Kate Greenaway dresses; elderly rustics tending to fragrant gardens; glassy eyed children staring in wonder at the unfolding of the adult world. But it wasn't these sentimental watercolours that gave me my epiphany. Rather it was the modest black and white line drawings that accompanied each poem. These sharp bits of draughtsmanship captivated me, and led me to pick up a pencil and attempt – unsuccessfully – to match their economy of line.

Many others – especially professional illustrators – will have had similar formative experiences. Moments when the potency of illustration invades the soul; when the realisation dawns that drawing, painting and making pictures are what we want to do. Here again, is a similarity between writing and illustration. Writers and illustrators usually discover their talent at an early age. The facility to write prose and draw pictures isn't something we discover aged 19 – we discover it much earlier, usually in infancy.

And it's this sense of illustration being connected to our personal development that makes it such a vivifying force. It may be facing one of its most testing periods, but illustration has a place in the hearts and minds of countless individuals; a quality that makes it one of the most important and enduring of the visual arts.

Advertising

Judges

Alex Bamford[1]
Senior Art Director, RKCR/Y&R

Alex has been an art director since leaving college in Cornwall over 20 years ago. He intends to continue working in advertising until he stops getting a thrill from seeing artwork he's commissioned. That could be some time.

"I love illustration. As an art director who is apt to be rather too hands-on, I love the enforced hands-offness of it all. The strongest work in this section felt pure and uncompromised. Well conceived, well briefed and well left alone."

Angelo Ferrara[2]
Senior Director, Wolff Olins

Angelo is Senior Director at Wolff Olins. He has vast experience in directing and producing projects in different markets and industry sectors from re-branding electrical goods companies to high street fashion. Clients included: Sen-Hutchison Whampoa, Yacht-Randstad, Toyota, Indesit, M-real, Madeira Island, Booths.

Prior to joining Wolff Olins, Angelo worked for Italia/BBDO working on events and social editorial proje cts for major Italian design companies such as Pininfarina and Gae Aulenti for Snaidero Group, the Coupé Fiat launch for Gruppo Fiat and an event with Amnesty International for Tian An Men.

In 1994, he represented Italy on the 'Mediterranean European Designer' in Portugal and one of his project for the Italian tourism office (the biggest chair in the world) is now in the Guinness book of world records.

Angelo also teamed up with Oliviero Toscani on a sculpture that became the symbol for an international convention in Italy.

Jackie Lynch[3]
Project Manager, Art Buyer, BBH

Jackie started working for BBH in February 2004 and has held the position of Project Manager/Art Buyer since 2005.

Her hobbies include visiting the theatre, exhibitions and yoga as well as being a keen member of a dinner/book club!

"I thought there were some interesting entries - I thought some were really beautiful although overall didn't feel I saw anything really different or distinct."

Mary Martin[4]
Art Buyer, AMV BBDO

Mary has been an Art Buyer at AMV BBDO Ltd for six years. Prior to joining AMV BBDO Ltd she worked as a Stills Producer.

"I was impressed by the high standard and diversity of the illustrations entered into the awards."

Simon Pedersen[5]
Art Buyer, AMV BBDO

After completing his BA(hons) and Post-Graduate degree in Fine Art, Simon started his career as an Art Buyer at Publicis, where he spent 5 years commissioning photographers and illustrators to undertake global advertising campaigns for numerous clients. Currently, Simon is one of the Art Buyers at Abbott Mead Vickers BBDO where he continues to commission Illustration, design and photography on a daily basis.

GOLD

Andy Potts
Birds

Medium	**Digital**
Brief	**To create an image for an IBM print ad to promote a new global business innovation campaign entitled 'What Makes You Special?'.**
Commissioned by	**Mike Hahn**
Client	**Ogilvy**
Commissioned for	**IBM**

Hailing from Dudley in the UK, Andy graduated with a BA Hons in Illustration from Portsmouth University in 1995. Soon after he moved to London and partnered up with an Apple Mac to pursue dual careers in new media and freelance illustration. Since then the commissions have flown in, ranging from advertising, book covers and editorial spots in newspapers and magazines for a wide range of international clients. His style is an energetic fusion of traditional and new techniques, where hand crafted elements collide with digital collage, 3D and photography with colourful results. He is also a member of UK illustration collective Black Convoy and has recently designed murals and exhibited work with fellow illustrators for online gallery 4WALL. Andy also works with motion graphics and has created feature film titles and numerous DVD menu interfaces during his seven-year stint as Lead Designer at award winning DVD studio Abbey Road Interactive.

Clients include IBM, Ogilvy, McCann Erickson, Wired, Random House, Brahma Beer, New York Post, British Transport Police, Microsoft, Newsweek, Time (Europe), Premiere, TBWA/GTT, Museum Of London, 23Red, Boston Globe, MIT Tech Review, Channel 4, The Advocate, Morrow Peak Snowboards, Time Out London, Fast Company, The Guardian, The Observer, The Independent, The Economist.

1 Winning illustration
2 Sketch
3 On billboard
4 Preperation illustrations
5 Final Finished Poster

11

SILVER

Ashley Potter
Care Poster

Medium	**Mixed/digital**
Brief	**Poster in the style of the associated animated film celebrating 60 years of the charity "Care International".**
Commissioned by	**Mario Cavalli**
Client	**Th1Ng Corp Ltd**
Commissioned for	**BBDO Campaign Berlin**

Ashley Potter graduated from St Martin's School of Art in 1982.

He had work accepted in Images and other European Illustration Annuals. Signed on the dole and sought work in the world of illustration. Artist Partners Illustration Agency agreed to represent him and he was commissioned by Penguin to produce book jackets for Thomas Wolfe's four American classic novels. In 1984, he won Images 9 "Best Newcomer" award and a variety of jobs followed in editorial, publishing and design.

In addition to his commercial work, Ashley took part in several group exhibitions and three solo shows throughout London, i.e. at the Monolith Gallery, Soho; Zanzibar, Covent Garden; The Torture Gardens, Islington.

He moved into animation and commercials design and art directed the award wining 'Soho Square' with director Mario Cavalli for Channel 4's Animate series and won a BAFTA and an Emmy for the animated version of Chaucer's Canterbury Tales. He art directed the Care International film, which this poster relates to and which was selected for this year's British Animation Awards.

Ashley is currently Programme Leader of the Design: Illustration course at the University of Plymouth, as well as a freelance illustrator.

1 Winning illustration
2 Sketches

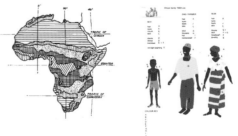

BRONZE

Jonathan Burton
Parade

Medium	Pen and ink (line and wash)
Brief	Promotional image for illustration agent NB Illustration.
Commissioned by	Charlotte Berens
Client	Nb Illustration
Commissioned for	Nb Illustration

Since graduating from Kingston University in 1999 with a MA, Jonathan has worked as an illustrator for such clients as the BBC, BMW/Mini, The Guinness Book of Records, Saatchi & Saatchi, Toyota, Time Magazine, The Times, Esquire, GQ and a whole bunch of others in Europe, USA and Australia.

He has recently been awarded Silver in the 3D Illustration Show at the Society of Illustrators in New York as well as being recognized by American Illustration, 3x3 Magazine and the 3x3 pro show Annual.

The Parade drawing for NB Illustration is inspired by the members of the agency and their eclectic tastes in music, fashion, their favourite animals and personal heroes.

13

1 Winning illustration
2 Sketches

Portrait: Oscar Walton

Books

Judges

Nathan Burton [1]
Senior Designer, Penguin Books
Nathan Burton is a senior designer at Penguin books looking after the Hamish Hamilton imprint. He started his career in book jacket design at Bloomsbury Publishing in 1998.

"I found the entries quite varied, from the few pieces that were incredibly exciting to the more mundane pedestrian work. Illustration feels like a healthy industry to be working in at the moment especially in publishing with the amount of commissions far outweighing that of photography."

Jeremy Butcher [2]
Art Director, Simon and Schuster
Since graduating from Bath College of Art, Jeremy has been designing book covers for sixteen years working for Longman, Dorling Kindersley, Random House, Transworld and currently as Art Director at Simon and Schuster.

"Illustration is being used more frequently on book covers recently. There seems to be a demand for fresh, hand-done crafted work."

Eddie Rippeth [3]
Primary Literacy Publishing Manager, Nelson Thornes
Eddie is an exiled Geordie who has worked as an editor and publisher in children's educational books for over a decade except for six months spent travelling around the world. His pride and joy in that time has been the Collins Big Cat guided reading series, in which he worked on the commissioning and editing of over 150 full colour reading books involving dozens of wonderful artists such as Tony Ross, Nick Schon, Bee Willey, Scoular Anderson, Guy Parker-Rees, Nick Butterworth, Tim Archbold and many, many more of similar calibre. In 2007, he has taken up a new job with Nelson Thornes where he hopes to be publishing top quality reading books soon! He is married to Judith and has two young daughters, Sophie and Imogen.

"I thought the entries were of a terrific standard and I was greatly impressed by the sheer range of styles, even if some weren't to my taste. Choosing a winner was very difficult, and it was very close with the final five - I think if it had been a different day I may have submitted a different winning order! It's been a great honour to do this for the AOI - I was awestruck by your list of patrons."

Robbin Schiff [4]
Executive Art Director, Random House NY
Robbin Schiff is the Executive Art Director at the Random House Trade Publishing Group in New York City. For more than 20 years, she has enjoyed designing book jackets that incorporate illustration. Last year, in her first experience in the editorial role, she published an illustrated book called Envelopes by the British illustrator Harriet Russell.

Illustration on book covers in the States seems to be enjoying a resurgence after a long drought in which only a few styles for certain categories would be considered appropriate.

"After the long prevalence of photographic imagery, there seems to be a reverse trend towards using more stylized and distinctive illustrations to package books."

Roger Walton [5]
Art Director, Duncan Baird Publishers
Roger Walton is currently Art Director of Duncan Baird Publishers. Before joining DBP he worked for a number of companies including Mitchell Beazley, The Observer Newspaper and Davenport Associates as well as running his own design company, Roger Walton Studio.

CWA Silver Dagger Award Winner

Morag Joss

Author of
Half Broken Things

PUCCINI'S GHOSTS

a novel

1	3	**1** Finished Cover
2		**2** Sketches
		3 Winning illustration

GOLD

Christopher Gibbs
Puccini's Ghosts

Medium	**Digital**
Brief	**Illustration for the cover of "Puccini's Ghosts" by Morag Joss.**
Commissioned by	**Jamie Warren-Youll**
Client	**Bantam Books**

Christopher Gibbs gained a first class honours degree in illustration at Norwich School of Art and Design, followed by a postgraduate diploma from the University of Brighton. After working at Arena illustration agency for 2 years, he became freelance in 2000 and has since worked for various clients in the UK and USA, producing images for book covers and magazines. He has exhibited his work at the EICH Gallery in Hull, and has been a visiting lecturer for illustration in Norwich. He lives in High Wycombe, with his dog and an infinitely more obedient Apple Mac.

'A book about pleasure, the pleasure of
cooking, eating, sharing and reading'
Guardian

SILVER

Alice Tait
Real Cooking - Nigel Slater

Medium	Pencil, dip-pen and ink
Brief	Design and illustrate front and back cover for Nigel Slater; brief requested a feeling of a personal and sensitive approach to cooking and getting down to basics. It also needed to set an arresting visual format which could be applied to a series.
Commissioned by	John Hamilton
Client	Penguin Books

London based illustrator Alice Tait left art college in Bath 5 years ago and has been earning a living from drawing ever since.

Alice is inspired by the verve and pace of London, carrying her sketchbook everywhere to record the faces of strangers, cake shop windows and seedy pigeons. When not spying on people on the tube she can be found at her space at Great Western Studios elbow deep in ink and old type books.

Her clients include British Airways, Jamie Oliver, Penguin Books, The Times, The Drawbridge, Vogue and XFM.

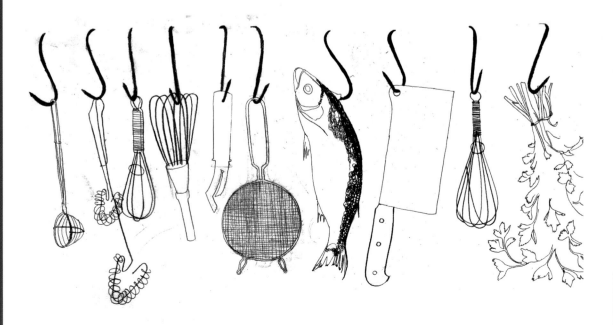

| | 1 Winning illustration |
| 2 Sketch |
| 3 Work in progress |

BRONZE

Paul Boston
Penguins Stopped Play

Medium	**Digital**
Brief	**To depict an arctic penguin pitch-invasion, a penguin making off with the ball and a whale in the background.**
Commissioned by	**Sara Marafini, Art Director**
Client	**John Murray Publishers**

After 10 years in various bands playing round the West Country and the empty basements of London, Paul Boston knocked music on the head and went back to college. By the time he finally graduated and began work as an illustrator he was living in Brighton and it was 1998. Three years later, the DSS had to break the news to him that he was earning too much to get benefits. A year after that, he got his first (postage-stamp sized) weekly slot (in the Guardian magazine). Since those days he has produced pictures for all manner of clients on both sides of the Atlantic. After many adventures and years of steady progress, his work was included in the AOI's New Voices exhibition in 2006.

Paul currently lives in Bristol, up on a hill. From his kitchen window he can look across the old docks to the green hills of Somerset beyond. In his spare time he is working on a picture book entitled 'Dinosaur School', which will relate a small creature's adventures in some kind of Paleolithic educational establishment. He assures us that children everywhere will love it.

19

1 Winning illustration

2 Sketch

3 Sketch

Design &
New Media

Judges

Mike Ferguson[1]
Creative Group Head, WWAV Rapp Collins
Age 40

"Illustration is back on top"

Nathan Gale[2]
Art Director, Creative Review
Nathan Gale has been art director of leading monthly communication arts journal Creative Review for almost nine years. During that time he has redesigned the magazine twice, once to mark the magazine's 20th anniversary and more recently in 2005. Gale is the author of Type 1, a book devoted to showcasing the best of digital typeface design published by Laurence King in 2002. He also runs design studio Intercity, which he set up with two other partners in 2004.

"I did actually like the website - it gave me a chance to sit down when I had a quiet hour or two and really look at the images. In general, I thought the standard of work was fairly good... But for me, my favourites really stood out - it was easy to recognise the best work, which is testament to the winners - as they stood above the rest."

Carl Rush[3]
Founder & Creative Director, Crush Design
Established in 1998, Crush are a creative consultancy specialising in design, art direction, marketing ideas and advertising solutions for a broad range of clients in the youth, entertainment, music, fashion and publishing industries.

Rachel Veniard[4]
Designer, Browns
Rachel graduated from Ravensbourne College of Design and Communication in 2002 and has worked at Browns for 4 years. Since joining Browns, she has worked on an array of varied projects for clients such as Fake London Genius, Invesco Perpetual, Design Council and Channel 4. Rachel has received a number of awards for her work whilst working at Browns.

Patrick Walker[5]
Designer and Illustrator, Dust Collective
Patrick Walker studied Graphic Arts and Design at Leeds Metropolitan University specialising in book design and typography. Following a few years in industry and academia, he spent a brief but enjoyable time at the RCA, leaving to set up the art/design collective Dust in 2000. Since then, Dust has produced amongst other things design and illustration for a wide range of commercial and arts based projects.

GOLD

Sarah Barnett

Peter And The Wolf 02

Medium	**Pen and ink, collage, cad**
Brief	**Hand-crafted album sleeve for folksy acoustic storytellers, Peter and the Wolf. A portrait of their eclectic musical styles and stories. Rootsy, ethereal, weird and wonderful.**
Commissioned by	**Gina Hewitt**
Client	**Skinny Dog Records**

Sarah attended Liverpool John Moores University, where, in 2004, she graduated with a BA (Hons) in multi media design. After showing her animation piece 'The Doodle' at The FACT in Liverpool, Sarah was asked to become a web designer at the Manchester based interactive agency Magnetic North. She spent two years working on projects with clients ranging from the BBC to Coca Cola. She also was a competitor in the Exposures Film Festival, where she again showed 'The

Doodle' animation at 'The Cornerhouse' in Manchester. After an offer to design the EP cover for the up and coming band 'Peter and the Wolf', Sarah realised illustration was her passion, and decided to follow a freelance career, leaving Magnetic North in August 2006. Since then, Sarah's illustration has gone from strength to strength and really become a much-loved obsession. She has worked on a wide range of projects and collaborations and also has regular commissions in 'Another Late

Night', a nationwide, monthly magazine publication. She is currently working on relocating to London, where she is looking to start a collective with her fellow designers, which will enable them to work on projects they're passionate about in the design and illustration industry.

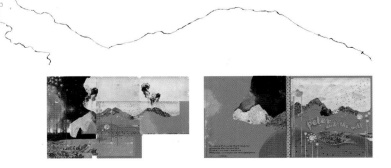

1 Winning illustration

2 Sketches & Preparation work

SILVER

Andy Smith

3 Colour Monster

Medium	**Digital**
Brief	**Create a monster with a special characteristic that can be used on a trading card.**
Commissioned by	**David Partington**
Client	**Peskimo**

Andy Smith graduated with an MA in illustration from the Royal College of Art in 1998 following a BA at Brighton University. Since then, he has worked as an illustrator in advertising, design, editorial and publishing with recent clients including Filofax, British Telecom, Nike, Expedia, The Guardian, Faber and Faber, Random House (US) and Bloomsbury. Aside from commercial work, he also enjoys combining his characters, stories and typography in an ongoing series of silkscreen printed books and posters. He works and lives in East London.

1 Winning illustration
2 Work in context

BRONZE

Mark Taplin
MTV's Sex, The Dirty Dozen

Medium	Mixed media digital
Brief	Create programme packaging for MTV's Sex, the Dirty Dozen including bumpers, astons and closer.
Commissioned by	Russell Hayer
Client	MTV Networks Europe

Mark completed an MA in illustration at Central Saint Martins in 1998.

Since then, Mark has worked as an illustrator/animator/designer for clients such as MTV, Vh1, Sony, Mother Advertising, Abbey Road Studios, Fallon, The Guardian, Intro, Imagination, John Brown Publishing.

Mark has a love for sequential story telling so animation has always been the next logical step for his work.

His first illustrated joke was published in the Topper comic and he got the bug from there on.

Influences come from comic artists such as Jack Kirby, Mike McMahon, David Mazzucchelli and Charles Burns.

Drawing has always been the core process of his image making.

On the 'The Dirty Dozen' Mark took control of the design/illustration and animation process from conception to final program packaging. This was an offshoot to MTV's 'The Virgin Diaries', which Mark also worked on but 'The Dirty Dozen' was an opportunity to make it his own.

In 2004, Mark has set up 'Taplabs' as an umbrella for all his work including his collaborative work. He is also a founder/active member of illustration collective Black Convoy and has made a illustrated/animated self promo based around The Black Country 'Welcome to BeCountry' which has been shown in Europe and throughout the UK

1 Winning illustration
2 Sketches

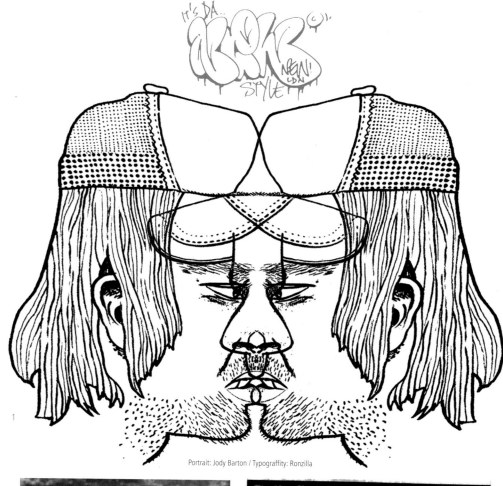

1

Portrait: Jody Barton / Typograffity: Ronzilla

2

4

Portrait: C.F. Payne

3

5

Editorial

Judges

Austin Cowdall[1]
Illustrator/Designer/Art Director, NEW Studio
Austin is a Graphic Artist/Illustrator/Designer/Art Director/Lecturer and founding member of the NEW Studio (TM). Through NEW he's worked on numerous high profile jobs from music projects to his trademark 'Brandalisation' illustrations (first seen in The Face, Dazed, Ldwn, The Guardian...), from D&AD winning M-real Magazines to a new series of Basics illustration books (AVA), and UK and worldwide exhibitions (V, Matsuri, BlackConvoy, onedotzero, 4Wall). He also produces and contributes to the internationally acclaimed Illustrated Ape Magazine.

"Viewing editorial on-screen is ok but it doesn't give a realistic or complete sense of the illustrator's skill unless you have seen the work in print before or unless you know the techniques used by the illustrator."

Pauline Doyle[2]
Art Editor, Guardian Weekend
Pauline has been Art Editor at the Guardian Weekend magazine for 3 years.

Before that she was at the Saturday Telegraph Magazine, and prior to that at Elle magazine. So she has a wide range of experience commissioning illustration from the fashion/style led images required for a glossy to the fast-paced schedules of a newspaper supplement.

"When judging the illustrations for Images 31 I used the same criteria I use when commissioning: I look for an image which not only illustrates the story in an original way, but also 'holds the page' i.e. it is an interesting and arresting image in its own right. Any illustration contributes to the overall visual identity of the magazine it's published in - so I try to commission illustration that will stand alongside the best photography and writing, and not be secondary to it. The best illustration is always an image that is powerful in its own right - and that is what I looked for as a judge."

Etienne Gilfillan[3]
Art Director, Fortean Times
Etienne Gilfillan grew up in Montreal, mesmerized by comics and early American animation. He studied illustration and graphic design then moved to London, where he joined the Fortean Times (the journal of strange phenomena) as art director. With its offbeat content, the magazine is a brilliant showcase for illustration, championing new and unsung talent as well as many established international artists.

As well as designing the Fortean Times, Etienne regularly writes comics for Belgium's revered Spirou, collaborating with a new wave of talented, young European illustrators.

"Editorial illustration is only partially about graphic skill. The illustrator's ability to come up with amazing ideas and cleverly solve a brief is as invaluable a talent as a distinctive graphic style. This year's winner demonstrates this combination perfectly."

Steven Heller[4]
Senior Art Director, New York Times
Steven Heller is a senior art director at the New York Times and co-chair of the MFA Designer as Author program at the School of Visual Arts in New York City. He is also the editor of VOICE: AIGA Journal of Design (http://voice.aiga.org/). He is the author, editor or co-author of over 100 books on design, popular culture and illustration. And he contributes to many magazines, including EYE, PRINT, Metropolis, Varoom, and Baseline. His website is: http://hellerbooks.com/

"The work was basically at a high level of competence but the innovations were few."

Anita O'Brien[5]
Curator, Cartoon Museum
Anita O'Brien has been the curator at the Cartoon Museum since 2003. Her work at the museum ranges from curating exhibitions, developing the collection - which ranges from Hogarth right up to present day cartoon and comic artists, organising events and workshops for both adults and young people, giving talks and other tasks too numerous to mention.

"In going through the entries I paid special attention to how the artist responded to the brief. I was especially taken with entries where the artist either interpreted the brief with wit and insight or brought out the tone or atmosphere of a story."

GOLD

A. Richard Allen
Twelve Drummers

Medium	Ink & digital
Brief	The Twelve Days of Christmas- Twelve Drummers Drumming.
Commissioned by	Gina Cross
Client	The Guardian

A. Richard Allen was born in Portsmouth in 1973, he grew up in Northamptonshire and spent much of his early adulthood in the care of Central Saint Martins College of Art & Design, London, first as a BA (Honours) Fine Art (Painting) Student, then as a reluctant administrator and finally as an MA Illustration student.

He escaped the gravitational pull of Central Saint Martins in 2001 turning freelance after a stint as an in-house illustrator with a doomed New Media company.

Since that time, A. Richard Allen has worked for a wide range of editorial clients (including The Times, The FT, The Guardian, The Telegraph, Reader's Digest, The New Statesman, The New York Times, Esquire) along with numerous design and advertising agencies.

A. Richard Allen lives in Bournemouth with his family.'

1 Work in context

2 Sketches

3 Winning illustration

SILVER

Simon Pemberton
Ghost

Medium	**Mixed media**
Brief	**To illustrate an extract of a short story based in a hotel with a ghost that prowls the corridors.**
Commissioned by	**Sarah Morley**
Client	**Independent Newspaper**

Born near Liverpool Simon moved to London to study BA Hons Design and MA Illustration at Central St Martins College of Art and still hasn't managed to get out again. Living and working in the East End of London keeps him busy with a studio next to London Fields and an extensive client list across Design, Publishing, Editorial and Newspapers both in the U.K and USA, but has been spotted north of Watford Gap, heading for the hills whenever possible.

Clients include Adobe UK, Fuji UK, New York Times, Guardian, Observer, Independent, Times, Mail on Sunday, Evening Standard, New Scientist, Condé Nast, VNU Publishing, Future Publishing, Reed Publishing, Penguin Books, Hodder Books, Harper Collins, Random House Publishing, BBC Worldwide.

Simon is also a previous winner of two Bronze awards in the Advertising and Design & Multimedia categories of Images and has been published in the 3x3 Best of Contemporary American Illustration.

Thanks must go to the designer on this job, who resisted the temptation to over complicate what needed to be a simple, bold and subtle image.

1 Winning illustration
2 Sketches

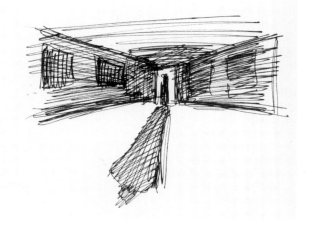

BRONZE

Laura Carlin
The Sins of the Fathers

Medium	**Mixed**
Brief	**The contact scandal - piece on children who have to visit their abusive fathers by law - often when they do not want to.**
Commissioned by	**Richard Turley**
Client	**The Guardian Newspaper**

Laura is a recent graduate of the Royal College of Art and mainly works within the medium of drawing. Whilst studying for an MA, the artist won several awards including the Shelia Robinson Drawing Prize, the Quentin Blake Award and the 2004 National Magazine Awards. She received the Uniqlo Fashion Illustration Awards in 2003 and 2004, which enabled her to travel to Shanghai. In 2006 Laura was awarded first prize in the V&A Illustration awards for Editorial Illustration.

The artist has exhibited her work in London, Paris, New York and Tokyo and has just finished illustrating a novel for Walker Books Publishers. As a commercial illustrator, Laura's work has featured frequently in publications such as Vogue, World of Interiors, The New Scientist and Condé Nast Traveller. Other clients include quality National newspapers, including The Guardian, The Observer, The Sunday Telegraph and The Independent. Internationally, she has worked for The New York Times, The Boston Globe and American Lawyer, having received a European Illustration Award for the latter. Recently, Laura had the opportunity to work on a much larger scale on advertising projects for clients such as British Airways, Trebor and Monsoon.

Additionally, Laura teaches part-time at a number of illustration courses, i. e. Central Saint Martins School of Art and Design or University College Falmouth. She is also a member of a committee initiated by Quentin Blake with the aim to establish the first illustration gallery in the UK in London, the Quentin Blake Illustration Gallery.

1 Work in context
2 Winning illustration

Self Promotion

1

2

3

4

5

Judges

Izhar Cohen [1]
Illustrator, Paris

Izhar has been an illustrator before he could pronounce the word. This profession has chosen him and keeps him off the streets. Illustrating provides him with a constant challenge: to maintain originality in his ideas and metaphors together with the search for new means of expression. He started his studies at the Bezalel Academy of Art in Jerusalem, followed by studies at the Ecole Nationale Supérieure des Arts Décoratifs in Paris and then at Central Saint Martins College of Art and Design in London. For more than twenty years, he is enjoying illustrating for newspapers, magazines, children's books and design companies throughout the world. He has been collaborating with The Times, The Guardian, Wall Street Journal, The Royal Mail, Walker Books, Dial, and many others.

"The process of assessing such a large body of work, so varied and of such high standard, called upon a thorough sharpening of my sense of judgment. I have found the experience simply inspiring. Overall, the images were visually coherent and varied in style. Despite the prominent use of digital media it is refreshing to see a fair amount of 'analogue' artworks. By nature, self-promotion works allow an artist to taylor his or her context, therefore, the dialogue between title and image have to be more carefully balanced by the author - preferably in a complementary manner. This wasn't always the case. Although illustrators are supposed to be authors of images whose purpose it is to communicate, the level of their abilities was very varied."

Helen Cowley [2]
Agent, Dutch Uncle

With more than 6 years industry experience, Helen embarked on a career as an artists' agent after graduating with a first class honours degree in Fine Art.

Working as an artists' agent with various creative management agencies, Helen has enjoyed a diverse and high-profile career.

Her experience has resulted in her working with some of the industry's leading talents for clients such as Playstation, Adidas, Royal Mail, Virgin, Perrier, VW and Audi.

Helen has been responsible for the rise of many illustrators' careers to date and continues to seek out passion within the artists she represents today.

Deirdre McDermott [3]
Picture Book Publisher, Walker Books

Deirdre studied Visual Communication at the National College of Art and Design in Dublin, she continues her apprenticeship at Walker Books (often heard to say: 'The more I know, the less I know') where she is the Picture Book Publisher.

Deirdre collaborates with illustrators, editors, designers and authors every single day in the pursuit of excellence in Picture Books (sometimes she is successful!).

"Although I'm used to dealing with illustration and artists in my day-to-day working life, I was quite disappointed (with a few obvious exceptions) by the triumph of style over substance in this self-promotion section of the awards."

Bob Mytton [4]
Partner and Creative Director, Mytton Williams Ltd.

Bob is partner and creative director of Mytton Williams (est. 1996). Prior to this, he worked with three leading London design consultancies: Pentagram, Williams & Phoa and Newell & Sorrell and taught graphic design at Bath Spa University.

With 20 years experience, projects have encompassed all aspects of design including visual identity, corporate and promotional literature, signage and packaging. Clients have included Andersen, Citizen Watch, Clarks, English National Opera, Environment Agency, Intercity, Niceday, Polaroid, Royal Mail, The Royal College of Dance and Waitrose. Awards include a DBA Design Effectiveness Award, D&AD, and medals at the New York Festivals. He is a fellow of the Chartered Society of Designers, and member of the International Society of Typographic Designers.

"Although there was some very good work and I enjoyed looking through it all, there was generally less innovation and originality in this section than I was expecting."

Hans Dieter Reichert [5]
Publisher, Co-Editor and Art Director, baseline

He has been Publisher, Co-Editor and Art Director of baseline – international typographics magazine since 1995. Over the years, he has worked with various eminent designers and design historians and illustrators such as the late Alan Fletcher, Ken Garland, Steven Heller, Stefan Sagmeister, Arnold Schwartzman OBE, to name just a few. Since 1993, Hans has also been a Director of the design company HDR Visual Communication whose clients include Rockport Inc., Phaidon Press Ltd., London Transport, Mercedes Benz AG, Norman Foster and Partners, The British Museum. Hans is a member of AGI (Alliance Graphique Internationale), an Honorary Fellow of the Graphic Biennale in Brno, a Fellow of the Royal Society of Arts and a Fellow of the International Society of Typographic Designers. He has won major design awards in the USA, UK, Europe and Japan. Hans has served as external assessor and lecturer at the Universities of Reading, Bath Spa, Northampton and in honour of his academic commitment, he has been awarded an honorary degree from the University College of the Creative Arts, South East England.

GOLD

Janet Woolley
Monkey Nuts

Medium	Digital
Brief	One of a series of autobiographical works.

1 Winning illustration

2 Sketches & Preporation images

In 1968 aged 16, Janet started full-time art education at a traditional art school, which focused largely on skills such as drawing, painting and craft based subjects. Having been informed there that she was an illustrator, she studied graphic design (specialising in illustration) at Brighton for three years, and in 1973 was accepted onto the Illustration MA at the Royal College of Art.

Janet graduated from the RCA with the Berger Award for Illustration, and although she was by no means arrogant, she wasn't prepared for the way her work was received.

Even then she was aware that one must compromise and work with others concerning content and the communication elements. She did feel that some art directors were trying to alter the very essence of her work and felt ill equipped to deal with this at the time.

For a period of around four years she exhibited and sold narrative paintings through art galleries and undertook private commissions.

In 1980, a drawing she had done for 'The Tin Drum' appeared in 'Design Magazine' with a short article.

And so it began.

In 1982, Janet won an Award in 'Sainsbury's Image for Today' competition followed by a Benson and Hedges Gold Award for Illustration in 1983.

She started being commissioned by Rolling Stone Magazine, Esquire, Washington Post as well as many British magazines such as The Sunday Times, Guardian and Radio Times.

In 1989, she was awarded the Society of Illustrators Gold medal for editorial illustration.

And so she has continued.

In 1985, she begun working as a visiting Tutor at Central Saint Martins, first on the BA Illustration and later on the MA.

In 1996, Janet was made a visiting Professor of Illustration.

In 1994, she won the D&AD award for Illustration in advertising. This was with work created for Bartle Bogle and Hegarty, advertising Murphy's Stout, and resulted in a number of advertising campaigns throughout the nineties.

Janet began to teach on the BA Illustration at Camberwell College of Art in 2001and, in 2005, became MA Illustration Course Leader.

She still works as a freelance illustrator and continues to create personal works of which this piece is an example.

SILVER

Matthew Richardson

Sexing The Cherry

Medium	**Mixed media**
Brief	**To illustrate the complex and surreal novel "Sexing the Cherry" by Jeanette Winterson, using a paper boat as a central icon.**

Matthew Richardson was born and brought up in London. He studied Graphic Design at Middlesex Polytechnic, followed by postgraduate study in Illustration at Central St. Martins. He recently completed an MA in Fine Art at UWIC (Cardiff). Inspiration or direction for illustrative work comes from a diversity of untamed, out-of-the-way places such as folk art, outsider environments, children's art, bric-a brac shops and the work of countless artists, currently a strange brew of Madge Gill, Cranach, Dubuffet, Tacita Dean, Jiri Kolar and Laura Ford.

He has worked for many and varied clients including the London Sinfonietta, Random House, Carling, Yellowhammer, Channel 4 TV, Penguin Books, Hodder Books, Radio Times, Quartet Books, The British Council, HarperCollins Books, The Guardian, MacMillan Books, The Sunday Times, World of Interiors, BT, Decca, EMI, WPP and New Scientist.

Alongside working to commission, Matthew also pursues and exhibits his own work, which utilises a diverse range of processes such as print, photography, drawing, the moving image, assemblage and various digital media. This work explores how objects and images become significant through recognition or misinterpretation and through changes in context. He looks at alternative histories, world views, myths and half-hidden stories.

1 Winning illustration

2 Sketch

BRONZE

Jonathan Gibbs
Tree, Birds and Fish

Medium	**Wood Engraving**
Brief	**To show the balance of nature within a frame.**

Jonathan trained at the Central School of Art and Design and the Slade School of Fine Art. His illustrations are made as wood engravings. As well as making prints, he paints and draws. Recently, he illustrated book jackets for 'Somewhere Else' by Charles Rangeley Wilson, Richard Mabey's 'Nature Cure' and 'Tiger in the Sand' by Mark Cocker, all for Random House. These involved various engravings of fish, birds and beasts with elements of landscape. Jonathan has continued to develop such themes in the studio. His agency, the CIA is brilliant and has represented him for many years with various kinds of work. As a recent example, he made some engravings for a 3D advertising campaign for Eblex, the government food agency. At the same time, there was a cover illustration for the Retired Parsons Handbook. This illustrates the range of tasks with which one may be confronted. Jonathan's last exhibition, 'Flint and Straw' at the Open Eye Gallery, Edinburgh, showed some of these engravings with larger oil paintings and drawings.

'Trees, Birds and Fish' is flattened, abstracted and reversed in sections of black and white, rather stylised but improvised in its composition. Jonathan began with a very loose pencil drawing, which became resolved as he cut the block. The idea is based on a cross, with elements above and below, in different worlds. There is always a particular composition in his mind, which tends to evolve in an intuitive manner as he cuts into the surface of the wood. This method enables him to carve and incise images, almost a sculptural process, and to make clearly composed pictures on a relatively small scale.

Illustration and teaching have given Jonathan the chance to explore drawing, literature and the graphic arts in a way rather differently from exhibition work; all of this resulting from freelance illustration and work with students. Jonathan is currently head of Illustration at Edinburgh College of Art, which is both inspiring and completely absorbing.

1 Winning illustration
2 Sketch

37

Critic's Award

The Erl King by Jenny Simms

Selected by **Steve Bell**

'Having studied them all the one I would like to choose is from the New Talent section, page 275, a digital collage by Jenny Simms of Southampton Solent University titled 'The Erl King'.

It is a very striking image that gets straight to the point. There was a huge amount of collage, both digital and manual to choose from, but surprisingly few pieces that used the potential of the medium effectively. What shines through in this piece is a classically simple selection and combination of elements to produce a very disturbing result.

All the work was of a very high standard, but some stood out for me, particularly Peter Ra (pp 68-71), Andy Smith (p24), David Grinsted (pp 242-3), Purdi Gibson (p195), Peter Hutchinson (p200) and James Fryer (pp 170-171).'

Steve Bell

Steve Bell was born in 1951 in London, raised in Slough, studied art in Middlesbrough and Leeds and worked briefly as a teacher in Birmingham before becoming a freelance cartoonist and illustrator in 1977. His original strip cartoon Maggie's Farm appeared in Time Out and City Limits magazines from 1979 until 1987 and, since 1981 he has written and drawn the If... strip in the Guardian. Since 1990 he has produced four large free-standing cartoons a week on the leader pages of the Guardian, which now appear in full colour. He created the memorable image of John Major with his underpants worn outside his trousers and of Tony Blair with Margaret Thatcher's rogue eyeball. His work has been published all over the world and he's won numerous awards, including the Cartoon Arts Trust Award eight times and the Channel 4 Political Humour Award in 2005. He has also received honorary degrees from the Universities of Sussex, Teesside and Loughborough. With Bob Godfrey he has made a number of animated cartoons for TV, including a cartoon biography, Margaret Thatcher – Where Am I Now? broadcast on Channel 4. He has had twenty seven books published, the latest being a cartoon autobiography of Tony Blair called "My Vision For a New You" published by Methuen. His work was recently part of an exhibition Tauchfahrten/Diving Trips - Drawing as Reportage at the Kunstverein in Hannover and the Kunsthalle in Düsseldorf. He has had retrospective exhibitions of his artwork at Sussex University in 1996, the Barbican Centre in 1999 and at Leeds University in 2006.

Jenny Simms graduated from Southampton Solent University in 2006 with a First Class Honours Degree in Illustration; she was also granted the Seawhites Award for Excellence in Studio Practice. Before graduating she had already produced commissioned work for a variety of organisations, including the national government agency, JISC.

As her mother is originally from Iceland, Jenny takes some of her magical creativity from her Icelandic roots, as well as her rural childhood spent in the British countryside. More recent influences are taken from the writings of Angela Carter and Jenny's own interest in the darker side of fairytales.

Jenny's passion for digital illustration grew from her initial experimentation with the media whilst she was studying for her degree. She likes to use this technology to manipulate her drawings, paintings and photographs into sometimes complicated layered imagery.

Jenny pursues her own work in her free time and exhibits it on her website at www.jennysimms.com. She also spends time experimenting with and expanding her knowledge of other digital applications.

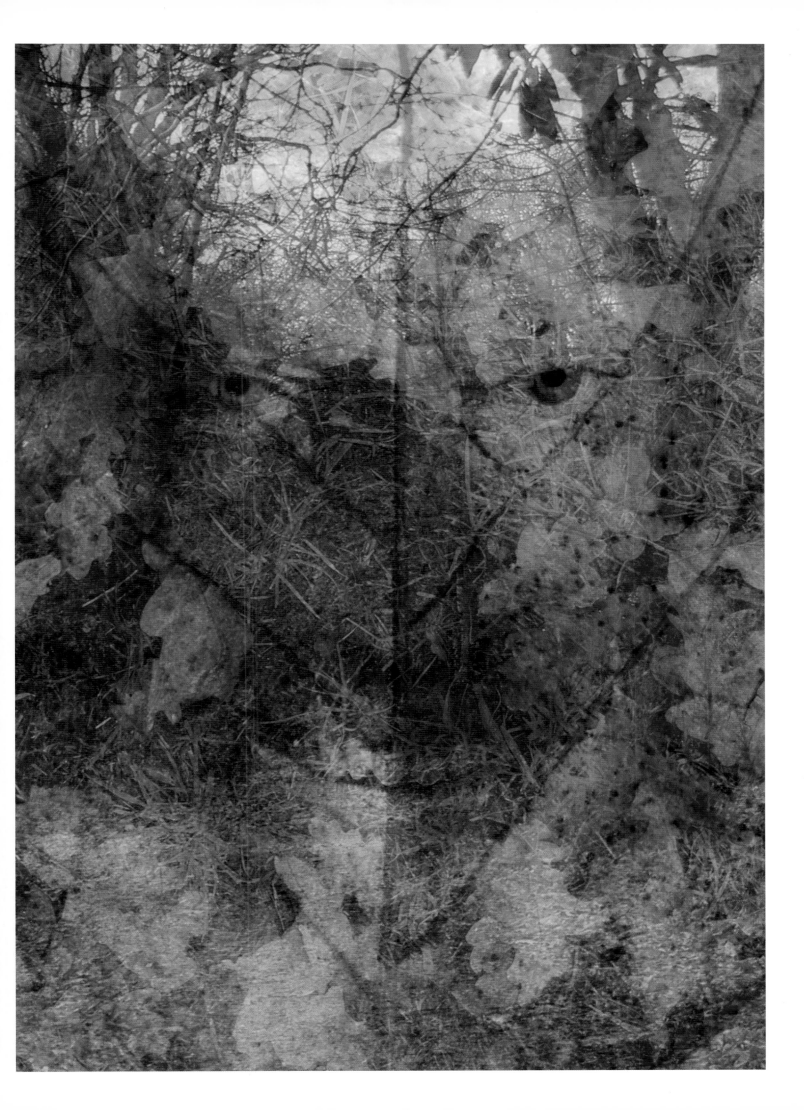

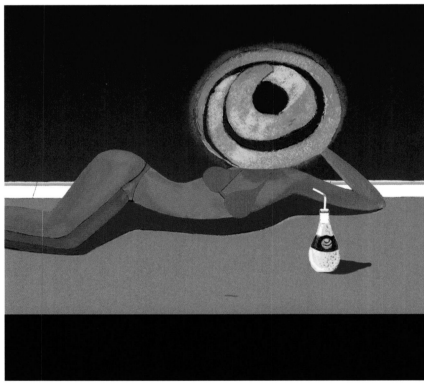

David Mcconochie
Deja Vu

editorial

Medium	Digital
Brief	Create an image that captures the feeling of Deja Vu and the theory that it is caused by so called "trigger memories".
Commissioned by	Steve Marsh
Client	BBC-Bristol Magazines Ltd

Eleanor Clark
Untitled

advertising

Medium	Acrylic on paper, digital
Brief	Illustrate woman sunbathing by pool, must compliment the Orangina logo, to sit alongside on new Orangina bottle.
Commissioned by	Philippa Dunning
Client	23 Red
Commissioned for	Orangina

Ridade Al-Daghestani
Passionate Dancer

self-promotion

Medium	Digital
Brief	An illustration from a mythological story that I wrote, entitled: 'Flow: Earthing the Ground', it's about a Circassian dancer named Amazeia.

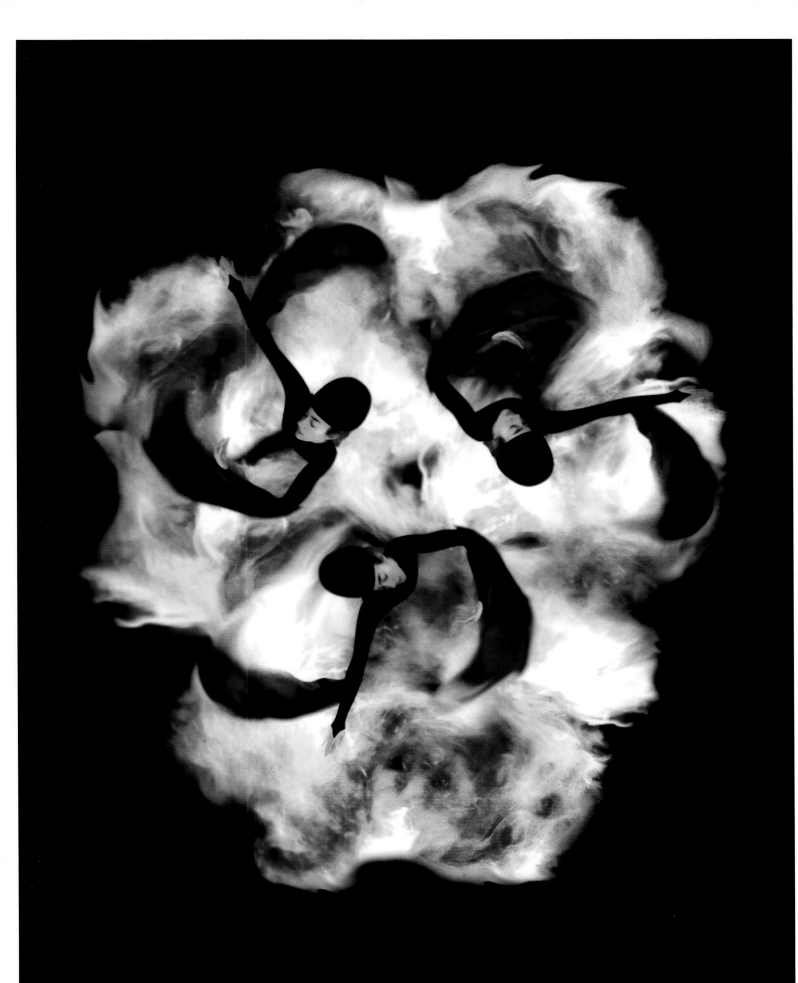

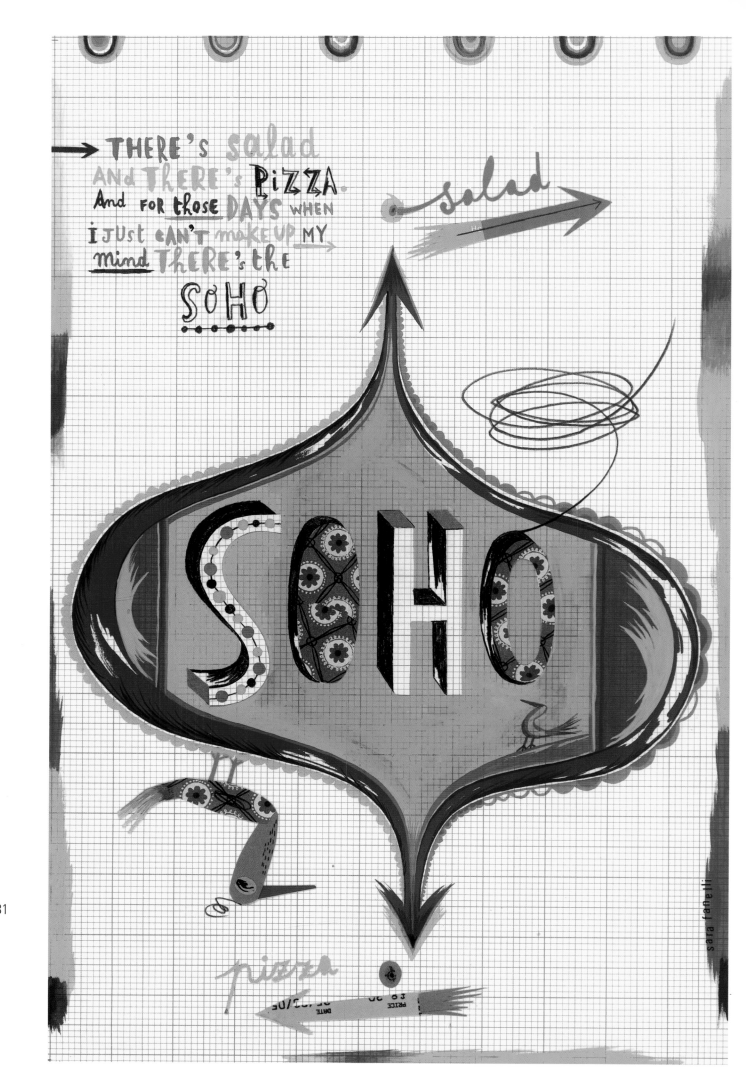

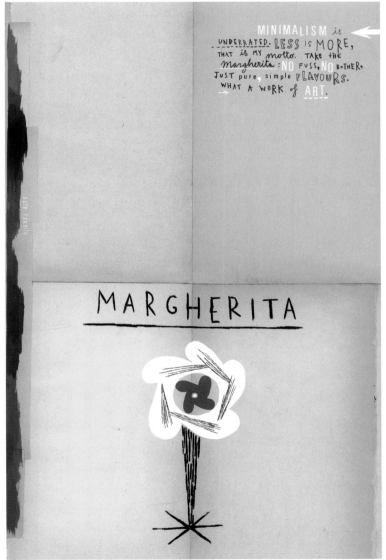

MINIMALISM *is* UNDERRATED. LESS IS MORE, THAT IS MY *motto*. TAKE THE *Margherita* : NO FUSS, NO BOTHER, JUST *pure*, simple FLAVOURS. WHAT A WORK OF ART.

MARGHERITA

My daughter says I should ACT my AGE.

	Sara Fanelli			**Sara Fanelli**
	Soho			Margherita
	design			**design**

Medium	Collage	
Brief	Cover for Pizza Express menu. The copy I had to illustrate is included in the image. Title: (Pizza) Soho.	
Commissioned by	Tamsin Loxley	
Client	The Nest/Pizza Express	

Sara Fanelli
Soho
design

Medium · Collage
Brief · Cover for Pizza Express menu. The copy I had to illustrate is included in the image. Title: (Pizza) Soho.
Commissioned by · Tamsin Loxley
Client · The Nest/Pizza Express

Sara Fanelli
Margherita
design

Medium · Collage
Brief · Cover for Pizza Express menu. The copy I had to illustrate is included in the image. Title: (Pizza) Margherita.
Commissioned by · Tamsin Loxley
Client · The Nest/Pizza Express

Sara Fanelli
Fiorentina
design

Medium · Collage
Brief · Cover for Pizza Express menu. The copy I had to illustrate is included in the image. Title: (Pizza) Fiorentina.
Commissioned by · Tamsin Loxley
Client · The Nest/Pizza Express

 Katherine Baxter
Pompeii
self-promotion

Medium	**Watercolour and pen**
Brief	**Double page spread from a proposed book about a story of a Villa in Pompeii.**
Commissioned by	**Mike Davis**
Client	**Kingfisher**

Christopher Gibbs
Natural Mandala

books

Medium | **Digital**
Brief | **Illustration for a book on Mandalas, "Meditations to help you find peace and awareness in the Beauty of Nature".**
Commissioned by | **Manisha Patel**
Client | **Duncan Baird Publishers**

Stanley Hooper
Housing Energy Pack

editorial

Medium | **Mixed media**
Brief | **To produce an image illustrating the possible introduction of a home buyers energy pack to show energy efficiency of houses.**
Commissioned by | **Liz Couldwell**
Client | **The Guardian**

Jennifer Lam
City Of Imagination

books

Medium | **Mixed media**
Brief | **To depict an imaginary street scene, Mong Kok (Hong Kong) for the back cover of the book 'City Of Imagination' by Michael Ingham. The author was looking for creative illustration work for his book about imagination and images of Hong Kong.**
Commissioned by | **Michael Ingham**

Satoshi Kambayashi
Panic Over Bird Flu

editorial

Medium	**Digital**
Brief	**Reaction over bird flu in Britain evokes the atmosphere of the Blitz era.**
Commissioned by	**Gina Cross**
Client	**The Guardian**

Christine Berrie
Don't Panic

editorial

Medium	**Coloured pencil**
Brief	**Illustration for a New Scientist graduate careers supplement entitled 'Don't Panic.'**
Commissioned by	**Craig Mackie**
Client	**New Scientist**

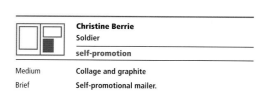

Christine Berrie
Soldier

self-promotion

| Medium | Collage and graphite |
| Brief | Self-promotional mailer. |

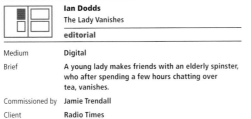

Ian Dodds
The Lady Vanishes

editorial

Medium	Digital
Brief	A young lady makes friends with an elderly spinster, who after spending a few hours chatting over tea, vanishes.
Commissioned by	Jamie Trendall
Client	Radio Times

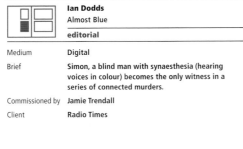

Ian Dodds
Almost Blue

editorial

Medium	Digital
Brief	Simon, a blind man with synaesthesia (hearing voices in colour) becomes the only witness in a series of connected murders.
Commissioned by	Jamie Trendall
Client	Radio Times

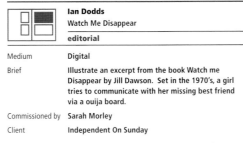

Ian Dodds
Watch Me Disappear

editorial

Medium	Digital
Brief	Illustrate an excerpt from the book Watch me Disappear by Jill Dawson. Set in the 1970's, a girl tries to communicate with her missing best friend via a ouija board.
Commissioned by	Sarah Morley
Client	Independent On Sunday

Frazer Hudson
More Energy + The Time To Enjoy It

advertising

Medium	Digital
Brief	Create a fishing scene using the Aranesp Pharmacceutical 'Red Blood Cell' logo as a fishing float. Also use Aranesp coloures Red, Yellow and Black.
Commissioned by	Eric Pernod
Client	Abelson Taylor
Commissioned for	Aranesp Pharmaceuticals

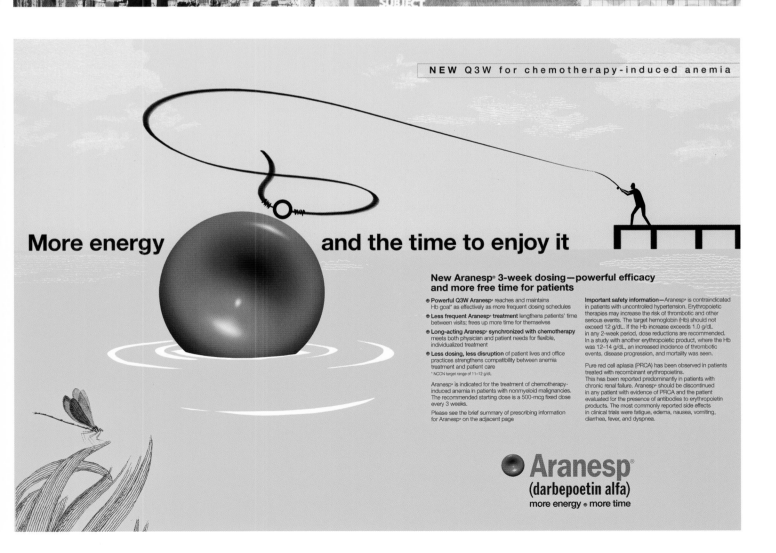

NEW Q3W for chemotherapy-induced anemia

More energy   **and the time to enjoy it**

New Aranesp® 3-week dosing—powerful efficacy and more free time for patients

- **Powerful Q3W Aranesp®** reaches and maintains Hb goal* as effectively as more frequent dosing schedules

- **Less frequent Aranesp®** treatment lengthens patients' time between visits; frees up more time for themselves

- **Long-acting Aranesp®** synchronized with chemotherapy meets both physician and patient needs for flexible, individualized treatment

- **Less dosing, less disruption** of patient lives and office practices strengthens compatibility between anemia treatment and patient care
  * NCCN target range of 11–12 g/dL

Aranesp® is indicated for the treatment of chemotherapy-induced anemia in patients with nonmyeloid malignancies. The recommended starting dose is a 500-mcg fixed dose every 3 weeks.

Please see the brief summary of prescribing information for Aranesp® on the adjacent page

Important safety information—Aranesp® is contraindicated in patients with uncontrolled hypertension. Erythropoietic therapies may increase the risk of thrombotic and other serious events. The target hemoglobin (Hb) should not exceed 12 g/dL. If the Hb increase exceeds 1.0 g/dL in any 2-week period, dose reductions are recommended. In a study with another erythropoietic product, where the Hb was 12–14 g/dL, an increased incidence of thrombotic events, disease progression, and mortality was seen.

Pure red cell aplasia (PRCA) has been observed in patients treated with recombinant erythropoietins.
This has been reported predominantly in patients with chronic renal failure. Aranesp® should be discontinued in any patient with evidence of PRCA and the patient evaluated for the presence of antibodies to erythropoietin products. The most commonly reported side effects in clinical trials were fatigue, edema, nausea, vomiting, diarrhea, fever, and dyspnea.

49

Aranesp®
(darbepoetin alfa)
more energy • more time

 John Bradley
School For Scandal

advertising

Medium	Ink/digital
Brief	Provide humorous illustrative interpretation of the Sheridan play 'School for Scandal'.
Commissioned by	Barrie Rutter
Client	Northern Broadsides

 Jake Abrams
Us

self-promotion

Medium	Silk screen print
Brief	One of an alphabetical Series–'Z-A' looking at relationships.

	Andrew Davidson
	Sabre Tooth
	design

Medium	**Wood engraving**
Brief	**To produce a set of 5 stamps based on Ice Age Animals.**
Commissioned by	**Susan Gilson, Catharine Brandy**
Client	**Royal Mail Group plc**
Commissioned for	**Royal Mail Philatelic Design Team**

	Andrew Davidson
	Cave Bear
	design

Medium	**Wood engraving**
Brief	**To produce a set of 5 stamps based on Ice Age Animals.**
Commissioned by	**Susan Gilson, Catharine Brandy**
Client	**Royal Mail Group plc**
Commissioned for	**Royal Mail Philatelic Design Team**

	Andrew Davidson
	Giant Deer
	design

Medium	**Wood engraving**
Brief	**To produce a set of 5 stamps based on Ice Age Animals.**
Commissioned by	**Susan Gilson, Catharine Brandy**
Client	**Royal Mail Group plc**
Commissioned for	**Royal Mail Philatelic Design Team**

Andrew Davidson
Woolly Rhino

design

Medium	Wood engraving
Brief	To produce a set of 5 stamps based on Ice Age Animals.
Commissioned by	Susan Gilson, Catharine Brandy
Client	Royal Mail Group plc
Commissioned for	Royal Mail Philatelic Design Team

Andrew Davidson
Woolly Mammoth

design

Medium	Wood engraving
Brief	To produce a set of 5 stamps based on Ice Age Animals.
Commissioned by	Susan Gilson, Catharine Brandy
Client	Royal Mail Group plc
Commissioned for	Royal Mail Philatelic Design Team

Jamie Cullen
The Ark

editorial

Medium	Digital
Brief	The Hammersmith Ark was an architectural triumph but is a commercial disaster.
Commissioned by	Richard Krzyzak
Client	Property Week

Lorna Apps-Woodland
Bird Flu

self-promotion

Medium   Collage

Brief   Create an image which reflects the bird flu scare and
its implications, speculative work.

Lorna Apps-Woodland
Ten Pound Dog

self-promotion

Medium   Collage
Brief   To design a CD cover for the band "Ten Pound Dog".
Speculative work.

Lorna Apps-Woodland
Gorilla Monsoon

self-promotion

Medium   Collage
Brief   A self promotional exhibition using the theme of
alternative superheroes.

Si Scott
If You Love Something

advertising

Medium   Print
Brief   "If you love something set it free" - what does this
mean to you personally. Freedom means something
different to each individual.
Commissioned by   Pete Lewis
Client   Fallon London
Commissioned for   Orange Communications

Kate Miller
Silverlands

books

Medium	**Digital**
Brief	**To illustrate the journey by Dervla Murphy across Siberia to Russia's Far East.**
Commissioned by	**Sarah Marafini**
Client	**John Murray Publishers**

Tobias Hickey
Stammering

editorial

Medium	**Mixed media**
Brief	**Difficulty in speaking soon becomes overlaid with anxiety and avoidance which can permeate every part of a child's life.**
Commissioned by	**Kevin Gray**
Client	**Times Educational Supplement**

Tobias Hickey
Sex Education

editorial

Medium	**Mixed media**
Brief	**New technology provides an interactive system to be acccessed privately by pupils and tune into messages that are culturally gender-appropriate.**
Commissioned by	**John-Henry Barac**
Client	**The Guardian**

Andrew Selby
Christmas Eve

design

Medium	**Digital**
Brief	**Produce a Christmas card image that acknowledges the traditional white Christmas but that gives a cosmopolitan and contemporary twist.**
Commissioned by	**Helen Usinn**
Client	**Die Illustratoren**

Alice Tait
Times Dine With Wine

editorial

Medium	**Inks and collage**
Brief	**Part of a series of illustrations to promote a Times 'Dine With Wine' offer, to show fun, spontaneity and sophistication.**
Commissioned by	**Guy Ivison**
Client	**The Times**

Alice Tait
Golborne Rd

editorial

Medium	**Oil patels and inks**
Brief	**Produce a series of illustrations which reflect the community for a local magazine.**
Commissioned by	**Ken MacDonald**
Client	**Goldborne Magazine**

Sarah Hanson
Travel Guide: Florida

self-promotion

Medium   Collage

Brief   To produce an image suitable for use as a
book cover for a travel guide on Florida, The
Sunshine State.

Sarah Hanson
Child Safety

self-promotion

Medium   Collage

Brief   My response to an article on child safety in
playgrounds and unwelcome onlookers.

Sarah Hanson
Travel

self-promotion

Medium   Collage

Brief   Produce an image that conveys/depicts the vitality
and importance of 'the new'. (Exhibition Piece).

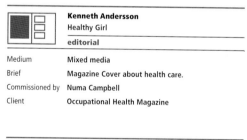

Kenneth Andersson
Healthy Girl

editorial

Medium	Mixed media
Brief	Magazine Cover about health care.
Commissioned by	Numa Campbell
Client	Occupational Health Magazine

Kenneth Andersson
Argentina

self-promotion

Medium	Mixed media
Brief	About wine from Argentina.

Kenneth Andersson
Cut Nose

editorial

Medium	Mixed media
Brief	Illustrating an article about what we say to our children to make them do what we want.
Commissioned by	Sarah Habershon
Client	The Guardian

Kenneth Andersson
Ironman

editorial

Medium	Mixed media
Brief	About men and homework.
Commissioned by	Sarah Habershon
Client	The Guardian

 Ruth Hydes
Café Bar in Florence

self-promotion

| Medium | Gouache |
| Brief | Visual diary of a holiday in Florence. |

 Sally Pinhey
Arisaema Griffithii

advertising

Medium	Watercolour
Brief	Botanical painting of plant specific to Himalayas in April.
Commissioned by	Renate Schwartz
Client	The Himalayan Connection

 Adam Graff
Alien Chicken

self-promotion

| Medium | Pen & ink, computer |
| Brief | One of a series of images created for a set of promotional books of things that I love and hate. |

pinkbald
scabbyta
lkingbag
gybellied
alienchi
ck en

65

	**Matthew Richardson**
	Eureka
	editorial

Medium	Mixed
Brief	One of three illustrations for a feature exploring the process of scientific breakthrough. Is it purpose, pattern or chance? Here, discovery is made through dreaming.
Commissioned by	Craig Mackie
Client	New Scientist

	Matthew Richardson
	Strange Enlightenment
	self-promotion

| Medium | Mixed media |
| Brief | A personal exploration and interpretation of the theme: Enlightenment. |

	**Matthew Richardson**
	Memories Of My Melancholy Whores
	books

Medium	Mixed
Brief	Cover for the novel "Memories of my Melancholy Whores" by Gabriel Garcia Marquez.
Commissioned by	Jon Gray
Client	Gray 318

Peter Ra
Churchill/Hitler

self-promotion

Medium   Digital

Brief   Speculative work on the relationship between good
and evil personified by historical figures.

Peter Ra

Jesus

self-promotion

Medium   Digital

Brief   Speculative work depicting the death of Jesus on
              the cross.

Peter Ra

Toxic London

self-promotion

Medium   Digital

Brief   Speculative work about the dangers of breathing
              carbon emissions in the city.

Peter Ra

Made In China

self-promotion

Medium   Digital

Brief   Speculative work on the subject of China
              emerging as a superpower and flexing its new
              economic muscle.

Peter Ra
Lucifer And The End Of The World
self-promotion

Medium | **Digital**
Brief | **Speculative work on the Apocalypse triggered by carbon car emissions.**

Peter Ra
Red Plastic Revolution
editorial

Medium | **Digital**
Brief | **To show a revolution within any form or any context.**
Commissioned by | **Javier Passo**
Client | **Belio Magazine**

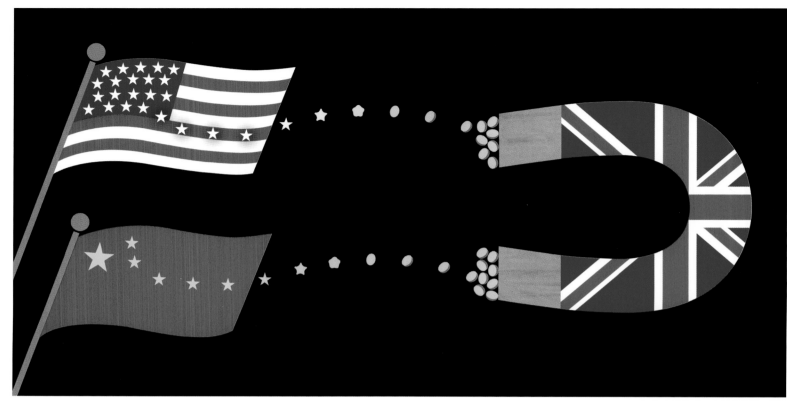

Gemma Robinson

Inward Investment

editorial

Medium	Digital
Brief	The UK is attracting competing inward investment from China and the US.
Commissioned by	Richard Krzyzak
Client	Property Week

Gemma Robinson

On Your Bike

editorial

Medium	Digital
Brief	Cycling holidays in France - the best way to eat and drink your way around the forests and vineyards of Alsace, without piling on the pounds!
Commissioned by	Maria Rodriguez
Client	Seven Publishing

Petra Stefankova

Hats, Cats And Dogs

self-promotion

Medium	Digital
Brief	Illustration to be mounted on original one-of-its-kind sketchel bag, a fashion accessory which people mostly carry in the streets.

Bee Willey

In The Princess's Cupboard

self-promotion

Medium	Mixed media and digital
Brief	To illustrate the inside of the princess's cupboard, containing possible outfits for the various functions she has to attend. The Princess would be aged between 6 and 11, approximately. Part of a book designed to be a guide on how to be a Princess.

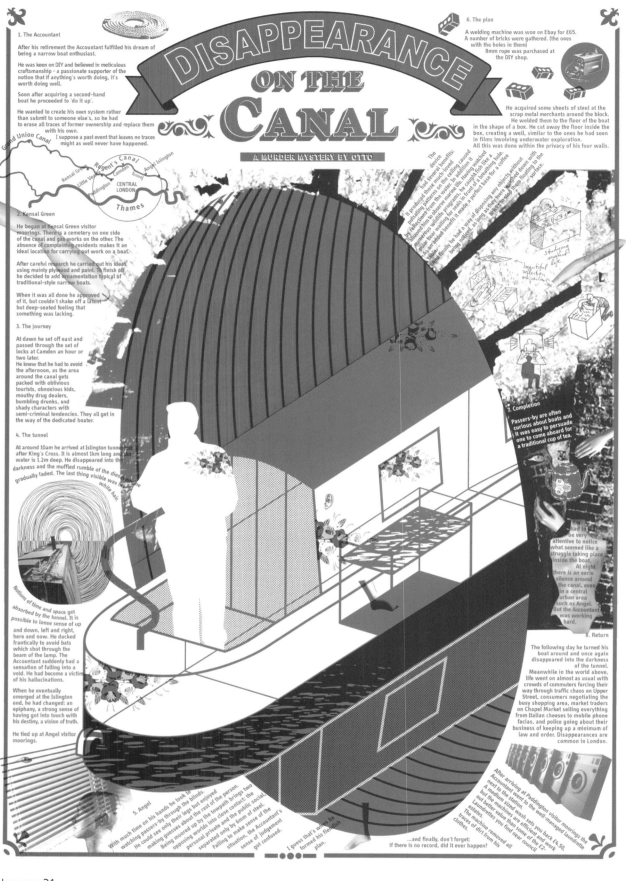

74 Images 31

Dettmer Otto

Disappearance On The Canal

self-promotion

Medium	Digital
Brief	Make a self promotional poster to be used on AOI publication.

Dettmer Otto

My Daughter's Husband Rejects Her Sexually

editorial

Medium	Digital
Brief	My daughter's husband rejects her sexually. They seemed the ideal match, but she has confided that she feels trapped in a sexless marriage. What can they do?
Commissioned by	Richard Turley
Client	The Guardian

Michael Worthy

Egocentricity

self-promotion

Medium	Digital montage
Brief	To construct a series of self-promotional pieces intended to establish a distinctive illustrative style.

Ian Pollock

Bird Flu Over the Cukoo's Nest

editorial

Medium	Ink
Brief	Topical subject for Saturday's Comment and Analysis page in the Guardian, the main topic being bird flu.
Commissioned by	Roger Browning
Client	The Guardian

Matt Murphy
The Conscious Carnivore

editorial

Medium	**Mixed**
Brief	**To produce illustrations to accompany the short story by Michael Pollen on the hunting of your own dinner.**
Commissioned by	**Arem Duplessis**
Client	**New York Times**

Matt Murphy
Costing the Earth

editorial

Medium	**Mixed**
Brief	**The effect of business on the environment.**
Commissioned by	**Sam Freeman**
Client	**The Big Issue**

Jenny Noscoe
Brazilian Tales From The Amazon

advertising

Medium	**Mono-print, pencil, Photoshop**
Brief	**Produce 30 images, one for each storytelling event. Target audience families. One colour tone image for print.**
Commissioned by	
Client	**Dorset Heritage Trust**
Commissioned for	**Sting In The Tale A Festival Of Stories**

Jonathan Burton

Undercover Economist

editorial

Medium   Pen and ink (line and wash)
Brief   To set the scene for an article based on an
                economist who spies on peoples eating and drinking
                habits on Londons' South Bank.
Commissioned by Sara Wadsworth
Client   Financial Times

Jonathan Burton

Boy Racer

editorial

Medium   Pen and ink (line and wash)
Brief   Portrait of racing car driver Colin Braun as a child.
Commissioned by Richard Eccleston
Client   Primemedia Group

Jonathan Burton

Mendelssohn

editorial

Medium   3d collage, photography
Brief   To Illustrate Felix Mendelssohn conducting
                characters from A Mid Summer Nights Dream.
Commissioned by Chris Barker
Client   Haymarket Publishing

Jonathan Burton
High Achiever

editorial

Medium	**Pen and ink (line and wash)**
Brief	**To illustrate article based on the effect that high achievers have on work collegues.**
Commissioned by	**Sam Wright**
Client	**John Fairfax Publications**

 Garry Parsons
How To...Look
editorial

Medium	**Digital**
Brief	An article exploring how everyone sees things differently because of their personalities. That in reality, people only see what they want to see.
Commissioned by	**Bruno Haward**
Client	**The Guardian**

 Garry Parsons
Bear In The Woods
self-promotion

Medium	**Mixed media**
Brief	Orignally a rough for Golf Digest Magazine USA about the consequences of hitting your ball into the woods.
Commissioned by	**Lauren Nadler**
Client	**Golf Digest USA**

9 ½ HATS

KANGOL SS2007

A SECLUDED APARTMENT ON THE OTHER SIDE OF TOWN.

TWO LOST SOULS DRAWN TOGETHER BY A SECRET PASSION.

HAT BOXES, WHIPPED CREAM AND BABY OIL STACKED TO THE CEILING.

IT COULD ONLY BE... '9 1/2 HATS'.

THIS SORDID TALE OF A MAN AND A WOMAN WITH A SERIOUS FETISH FOR HEADGEAR KNOWS NO BOUNDARIES, EXCEPT FOR ONE RULE... 'LEAVE YOUR HAT ON...'

JUST TRY NOT TO LOOK WHEN FRENZIED EMOTIONS ARE THRUST INTO OVERDRIVE AS OUR LID LOVERS DISCOVER AN OPEN REFRIGERATOR PACKED WITH KANGOL'S COOL NEW SPRING/SUMMER LINE (YOU DIRTY DEVILS, X).

82

Henry Obasi
9 And 1/2 Hats

design

Medium	Hand drawn and digital
Brief	A couple meet once a year in order to satiate their passion for headwear.
Commissioned by	Nic Hayes
Client	Kangol Headwear Europe

Victoria Rose
In A World Of Their Own

advertising

Medium	Mixed media
Brief	Create an eye catching original piece of artwork to advertise the design arcade in the official show guide. The original to be on sale at Grand Designs Exhibition along with a run of limited edition prints.
Commissioned by	Grand Designs
Client	Media 10 Limited
Commissioned for	Advertising The Design Arcade at Grand Designs 2006 in the official show guide

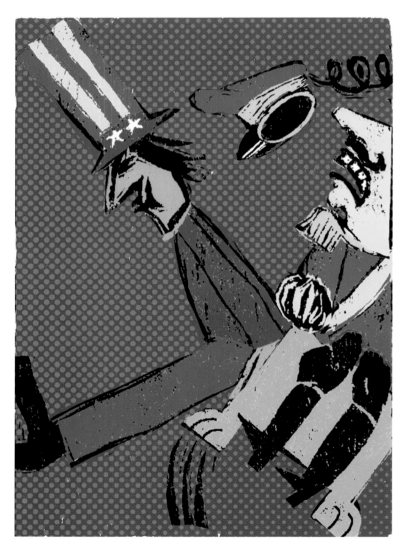

Daniel Pudles
The Price Of Intervention

editorial

Medium	**Woodcut and digital**
Brief	**A study on a century of American regime change, from Hawaii to Iraq.**
Commissioned by	**Fiammetta Rocco**
Client	**The Economist**

Daniel Pudles
Goodbye Isixhosa

editorial

Medium	**Woodcut and digital**
Brief	**South African constitution guarantees the parity of 11 languages. But English, mother tongue of only 9% of the population will soon crowd out the rest.**
Commissioned by	**Ayanna Prevatt-Goldstein**
Client	**Prospect**

Daniel Pudles
Kershaw's Diary

editorial

Medium	**Woodcut and digital**
Brief	**The Who second gig at Leeds University. An ex-student turned shepherd in Orkney gets two drumsticks and Daltrey's soaking towel after the final bow.**
Commissioned by	**Simon Esterson**
Client	**New Statesman**

Daniel Pudles
When Two Poor Countries Reclaimed Oilfields, Why
Did Just One Spark Uproar?

editorial

Medium	Woodcut and digital
Brief	The outcry over Bolivia's renationalisation and the silence over Chad's, betrays the hypocrisy of the critics.
Commissioned by	Roger Browning
Client	The Guardian

There's a whole **PARK** beyond the **OFFICE CHEESE PLANT**

COAL CELLAR

SNOW STORM

Normally the cat lives in the coal cellar and the polar bear in the snow storm, but today they decided to swap.

 Harriet Russell
Filofax Park Advert
advertising

Medium	Mixed media
Brief	Illustrated hand drawn lettering for filofax with a light, doodled quality.
Commissioned by	Suzanne Gaunt
Client	St Luke's
Commissioned for	Filofax

Harriet Russell
Cat And Polar Bear
books

Medium	Silkscreen
Brief	From own book titled "A colouring book for the Lazy" where every image is of black and white animals or objects.
Commissioned by	Marzia Corraini
Client	Edizioni Corraini

 Harriet Russell
A Brief Chapter In My Impossible Life
books

Medium	Silkscreen
Brief	Cover for a teenage fiction novel about an adopted girl who discovers her family roots and gets to know her birth mother.
Commissioned by	Patrick Insole
Client	Walker Books

87

Harriet Russell

Two Turtle Doves

editorial

Medium	**Mixed**
Brief	**To depict Two Turtle Doves as part of a specially commissioned series of illustrations for the Twelve Days of Christmas, featured each day on the Guardian letters page.**
Commissioned by	**Gina Cross**
Client	**The Guardian**

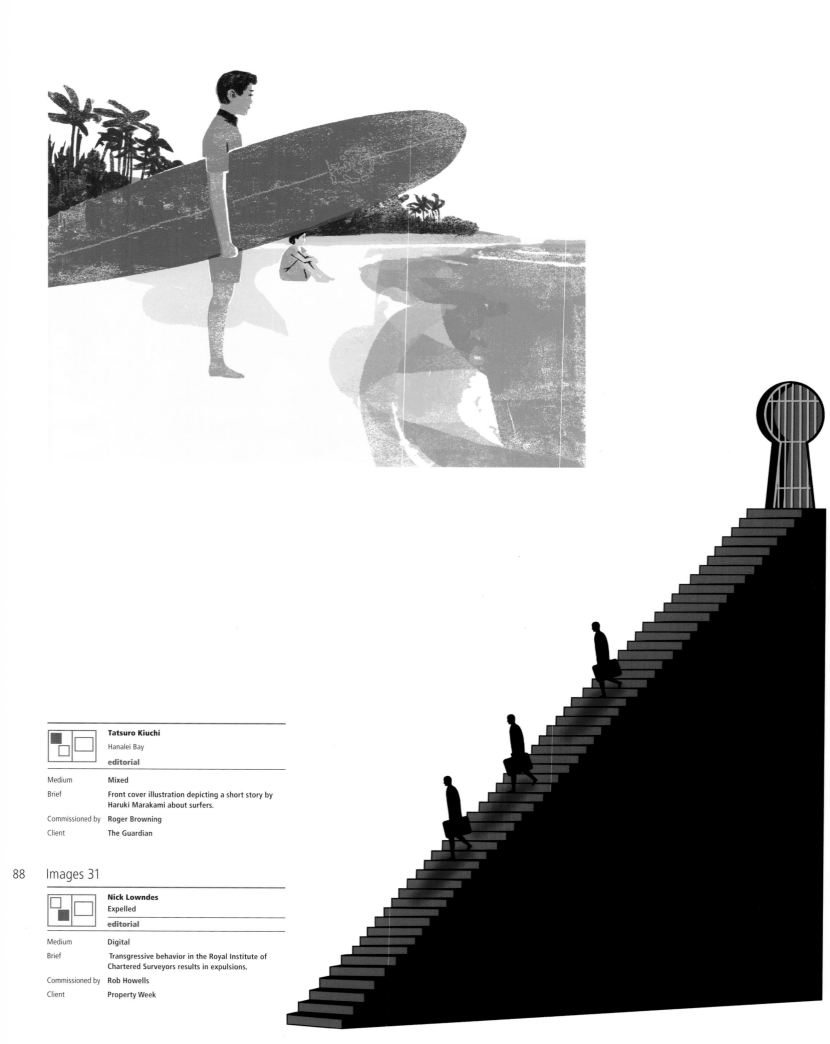

Tatsuro Kiuchi

Hanalei Bay

editorial

Medium	**Mixed**
Brief	**Front cover illustration depicting a short story by Haruki Marakami about surfers.**
Commissioned by	**Roger Browning**
Client	**The Guardian**

Nick Lowndes

Expelled

editorial

Medium	**Digital**
Brief	**Transgressive behavior in the Royal Institute of Chartered Surveyors results in expulsions.**
Commissioned by	**Rob Howells**
Client	**Property Week**

Per José Karlén
R&S Catalog Cover

books

Medium	**Digital**
Brief	**To create an image which reflects the spirit of the published books. The image shall appeal to both children and adults and encourage reading.**
Commissioned by	**Erik Tituson**
Client	**Rabén & Sjögren Publisher**

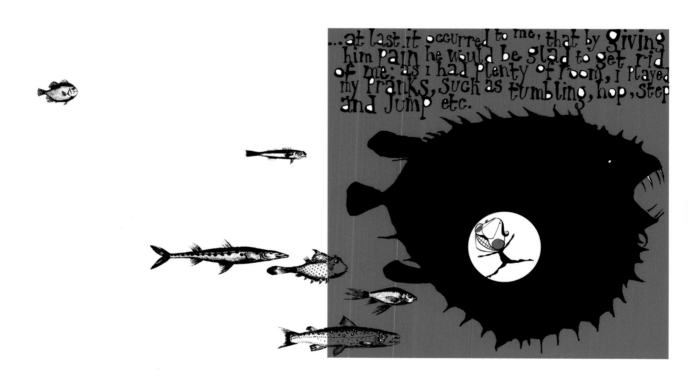

Stefan Isaacson

The Dark Side

editorial

Medium	Screenprint and acrylic on card
Brief	One person's account of clinical depression. The illness has gripped her grandmother, father, sister and best friend. "Sometimes, the urge to shake them is overwhelming".
Commissioned by	Bruno Howard
Client	Guardian Weekend

Emily Jepps

An Unexpected Companion

self-promotion

Medium	Mixed media
Brief	A double page spread from a children's book based on "The Surprising Adventures of Baron Munchausen" by Rudolph Erich Raspe.

Paul Withyman

Sleepers

self-promotion

Medium	Acrylic and matches
Brief	The painting is a response to the growing number of children who smoke and do not realise the damage that it can cause them.

 Stephen Knowles
Virus

editorial

Medium	Mixed medium
Brief	The theme was 'virus' - own creative interpretation.
Commissioned by	Nauko Leong/Dean Brand
Client	Riot (MTV) Magazine

 Stephen Knowles
Soya!

self-promotion

Medium	Mixed medium
Brief	Artwork produced after reading about the effects of soya plantations being the reason for increased global warming.

93

HELP US CHANGE THE MAKE-UP OF OUR FORCE

 Anders Westerberg
Sun Valley Tattoo

editorial

Medium	**Watercolour/digital**
Brief	**Sun Valley Tattoo Convention.**
Commissioned by	**Gillian Dundas**
Client	**Phoenix New Times**

 Andy Potts
Bumo

self-promotion

Medium	**Digital**
Brief	**To fulfill a brief to create a sport piece based on power, strength and speed to promote myself and Modart in techni-style sport magazine Ware.**

 Andy Potts
Help Us Change The Make-Up Of Our Force

advertising

Medium	**Digital**
Brief	**To create a visual to encourage more females to join the British Transport Police.**
Commissioned by	**Ana Jones**
Client	**Barkers Norman Broadbent**
Commissioned for	**British Transport Police**

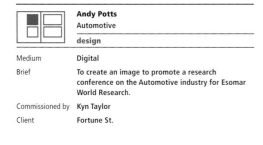

Andy Potts
Automotive

design

Medium	Digital
Brief	To create an image to promote a research conference on the Automotive industry for Esomar World Research.
Commissioned by	Kyn Taylor
Client	Fortune St.

Andy Potts
Business Crowd

advertising

Medium	Digital
Brief	To create an image for an IBM print ad to promote a new global business innovation campaign entitled 'What Makes You Special?'.
Commissioned by	Mike Hahn
Client	Ogilvy
Commissioned for	IBM

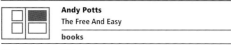

Andy Potts
The Free And Easy

books

Medium	Digital
Brief	To create a book jacket design for this Anne Haverty novel about upwardly mobile Dubliners.
Commissioned by	Eleanor Crow
Client	Random House

Andy Potts
Technology At Wimbledon

advertising

Medium	Digital
Brief	To create an image for an IBM print ad to promote the technology behind the 2006 Wimbledon Tennis Championships.
Commissioned by	Brigette Martin
Client	Ogilvyone
Commissioned for	IBM

Andy Potts
Flower Factory
advertising

Medium	**Digital**
Brief	**To create an image for an IBM print ad to promote a new global business innovation campaign entitled 'What Makes You Special?'**
Commissioned by	**Mike Hahn**
Client	**Ogilvy**
Commissioned for	**IBM**

 Andy Potts
Religious Evolution

editorial

Medium	**Digital**
Brief	Illustration for the Observer's book review section related to the evolution of religious thinking.
Commissioned by	**Chris Lupton**
Client	**The Observer**

Andy Potts
Buying A Pool

editorial

Medium	**Digital**
Brief	Illustration for an article about buying a luxury pool and the excessive amounts of money involved.
Commissioned by	**Jo Cochrane**
Client	**Inside Out Magazines Ltd.**

 Andy Potts
Working Fathers

editorial

Medium	**Digital**
Brief	Illustration for an article on fathers balancing their professional commitments to enable them to spend more time with their children.
Commissioned by	**Sarah Habershon**
Client	**Guardian**

Frank Love
7 Sins

self-promotion

Medium   Mixed/digital

Brief   Depict 7 deadly ingredient sins in the cocktails at
            'Dante's Bar & Grill'.

Daniela Jaglenka Terrazzini
Lady Purple And The Puppeteer

self-promotion

Medium   Mixed media
Brief   Image to illustrate a scene from 'The Loves of Lady Purple' by Angela Carter.

Daniela Jaglenka Terrazzini
Snow White Asleep In The Dwarves' House

self-promotion

Medium   Mixed media
Brief   Image to illustrate a scene from 'Snow White'.

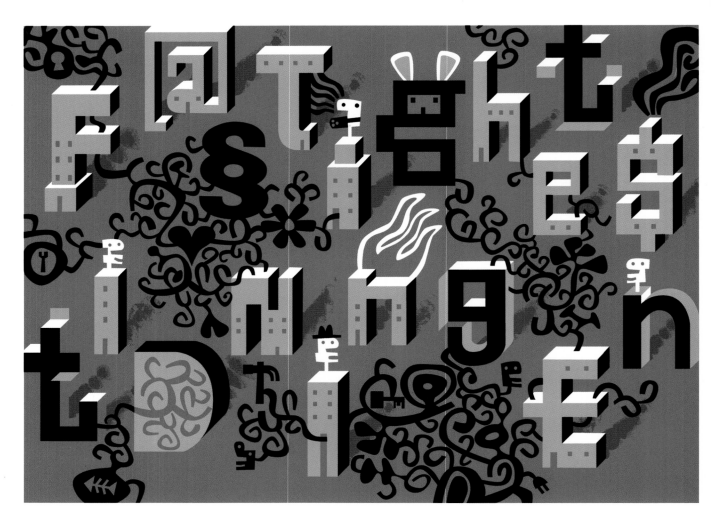

 Lasse Skarbovik / Stockholm Illustration
House

design

Medium	Computer
Brief	Cover for a brochure with information about the prizes and how to advertise in the magazine. The magazine is about and for house owners.

Commissioned by   **Cia Kilander**

 Lasse Skarbovik / Stockholm Illustration
Self Protrait

self-promotion

Medium	Computer
Brief	Abstract self-portrait.

 Lasse Skarbovik / Stockholm Illustration
Knee

self-promotion

Medium	Computer
Brief	My knee is an illustration I did after a knee infection.

Lasse Skarbovik / Stockholm Illustration
Seagate
books

Medium	**Computer**
Brief	**Cover for a book about outside technical innovations and accomplishments.**
Commissioned by	**Tim Shumann**
Client	**Little & Company**

Jay Taylor
Gender Blender

self-promotion

Medium   **Mixed media**

Brief   **How easy is it to change one's gender?**

Jay Taylor

Indie Kid

design

Medium	Mixed media
Brief	One of three illustrations for a Channel 4 website about youth tribes in Britain.
Commissioned by	Emma Warren
Client	Ramp Industry

Lars Rehnberg

Eskimo

self-promotion

Medium	Digital
Brief	Christmas card.

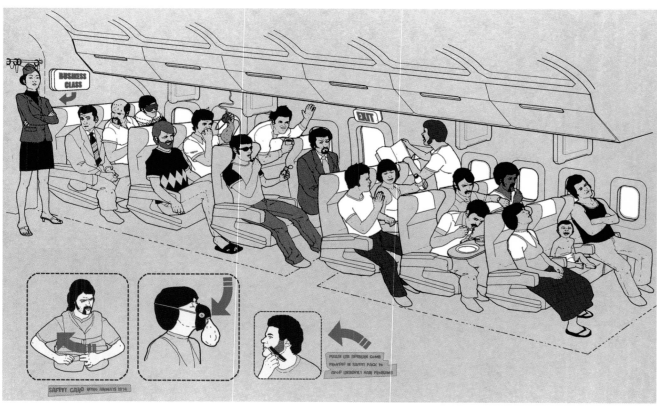

Lee Woodgate
How To...Use A Chemist

editorial

Medium	Photoshop/pencil
Brief	Weekly column about using a chemist. I highlighted waiting room with plastic chairs, nervousness of bird flu, embarrassment between sexes, silence, thrush (play on birds).
Commissioned by	Bruno Haward
Client	The Guardian Weekend Magazine

Lee Woodgate
What Is Wrong With This Picture?

editorial

Medium	Photoshop/pencil
Brief	Produce an illustration of diagrammatical crash cards combined with a scene, involving specific events to be highlighted in story. DPS illustration to have retro feel.
Commissioned by	Scott Bentley
Client	Natmag Rodale Ltd

Jasmine Mercer
Street Theatre

advertising

Medium	Acrylic
Brief	To produce an image which creates a dynamic identity for Poole Arts Festival, suitable to be used in promotional formats ranging from A1 to A6.
Commissioned by	Marianne Scahill
Client	The Arts Development Unit, Borough Of Poole
Commissioned for	Poole Family Arts Festival

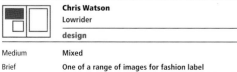

Chris Watson

Lowrider

design

Medium	**Mixed**
Brief	One of a range of images for fashion label "Unknown Pleasures". Low Riders were originated by Chicano customisers in East Los Angeles.
Commissioned by	**Steve Caton**
Client	**Unknown Pleasures**

Jonathan Williams

Cockroachus Historicus

advertising

Medium	**Photoshop**
Brief	To illustrate a natural history display cabinet with specimens lovingly collected and pinned down for scientific examination. Historicus has been brutally crushed.
Commissioned by	**Jonathan Richards**
Client	**Ecolab**

Sarah Coleman

Step Into A Story

design

Medium	**Pen and ink, digital**
Brief	Cover for Visit Britain's 'Storybook England' project, encouraging children to visit parts of the country which have inspired famous children's writers.
Commissioned by	**Adam Curry**
Client	**Liquorice**

Belle Mellor
Shaving

self-promotion

Medium	Pen and ink
Brief	Illustration on the theme of childhood, for a promotional book produced by my agent , Three in a Box.

Belle Mellor
Exclusion

editorial

Medium	Pen and ink / digital
Brief	For an article about the failure of the workplace to accommodate those with mental illness.
Commissioned by	Paige Weir
Client	Venture Publishing

Belle Mellor
Complex Problems

self-promotion

Medium	Pen and ink
Brief	For an article on dealing with complex problems (An alternative rough was selected by the client).

Belle Mellor
Copy-Write

editorial

Medium	**Pen and ink / digital**
Brief	**For an article on how the excessive use of copy-write in the US can restrict a writer's creativity.**
Commissioned by	**An Moonen**
Client	**La Times**

BEARD HALL OF FAME

Vicky Woodgate
Beard Hall Of Fame
self-promotion

Medium   **Digital**

Brief   A self promotional piece using wallpaper design and aged old images of famous or infamous people with BEARDS injecting a bit of fun and humour.

 Vicky Woodgate
Outside-Inside

books

Medium	**Digital**
Brief	**A future worth choosing living as one with nature, in harmony with the natural world.**
Commissioned by	**Phil Turner - 4Design**
Client	**Your Planet Needs You**

 Tony Healey
Norman Mailer

self-promotion

Medium	**Pencil**
Brief	**Preliminary drawing of the writer, Norman Mailer. One of a series of colour caricature portraits of literary figures.**

 Shonagh Rae
I Confess

editorial

Medium	**Digital**
Brief	**Lawyers were now required to confess all to the inland revenue regarding tax avoidance schemes.**
Commissioned by	**Richard Krzyzak**
Client	**Property Week**

 Miriam Latimer
5 Fruit And Veg A Day
self-promotion

Medium   Collage
Brief   Promotion for the Recommended daily fruit and
             vegetable intake i.e. 5 fruit and veg a day.

 Peter Horridge
Mozart And Shostakovich
design

Medium   Digital
Brief   A combined portrait image of Mozart and
             Shostakovich for the BBC Proms to be used on
             various promotional retail items in celebration
             of 250 years and 100 years since the birth of the
             composers.
Commissioned by Martin Premm-Jones
Client   Premm Design

 Peter Horridge
Butterfly Code
editorial

Medium   Pen and ink and digital
Brief   One of two images for a feature article and cover
             for New Scientist Magazine on the Butterfly Code,
             how messages can be hidden within a chaotic
             electrical or light signal.
Commissioned by Alison Lawn
Client   New Scientist

	Kevin Hauff
	Metropolis
	editorial

Medium	Digital / mixed
Brief	To Illustrate a BBC radio reinterpretation of Fritz Lang's film Metropolis, depicting the city as an iconic powerful and mythical environment.
Commissioned by	Jamie Trendall
Client	Radio Times

	Kevin Hauff
	Imagining Albion
	editorial

Medium	Mixed media
Brief	British science fiction has been imagining the future for over four centuries, but what does it tell us about our Island's past and our lost tomorrows?
Commissioned by	Hazel Brown
Client	Radio Times

	Kevin Hauff
	The Crucifixion
	editorial

Medium	Digital / mixed
Brief	Illustrate the Radio Times Good Friday TV page listings, depicting the Crucifixion of Christ covering the top and sides of the double page spread.
Commissioned by	Jamie Trendall
Client	Radio Times

	Mariko Jesse
	La Botella
	self-promotion

| Medium | Etching |
| Brief | To create an alluring image of a bottle for a group collection of cards in a Mexican Loteria game, with an Asian twist. |

117

Luke Knight
Uncle Sam

self-promotion

Medium	Acrylic, graphite, digital
Brief	To illustrate an article about America's seeming ignorance towards environmental issues.

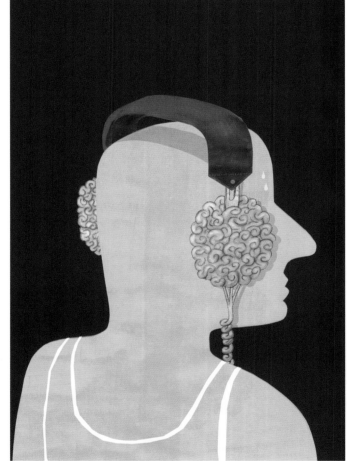

Luke Knight
Psychological Entrapment

self-promotion

Medium	Acrylic, graphite, digital
Brief	To illustrate the idea that one can be trapped by their own mind.

Luke Knight
In Two Minds About...

self-promotion

Medium	Acrylic, graphite, digital
Brief	To illustrate the idea of being in two minds about a decision.

Luke Knight
Self-Awareness

self-promotion

Medium	Acrylic, graphite, digital
Brief	To illustrate the notion that intelligent beings can be defined by their awareness of self.

Nancy Tolford
Tightrope Walker

self-promotion

Medium   **Digital**

Brief   **One of a series of works depicting different types of circus performers.**

Nancy Tolford
Evening In Spain

self-promotion

Medium   **Digital**

Brief   **Personal work from a travel journal.**

Nancy Tolford
Dance Palace

self-promotion

Medium   **Digital**

Brief   **Personal work inspired by a trip to the U.S.A.**

Nancy Tolford
Circus Star

self-promotion

Medium   **Digital**

Brief   **One of a series of works depicting different types of circus performers.**

Nancy Tolford
April Morning in Kyoto

self-promotion

Medium   **Digital**

Brief   **Personal work inspired by a trip to Japan.**

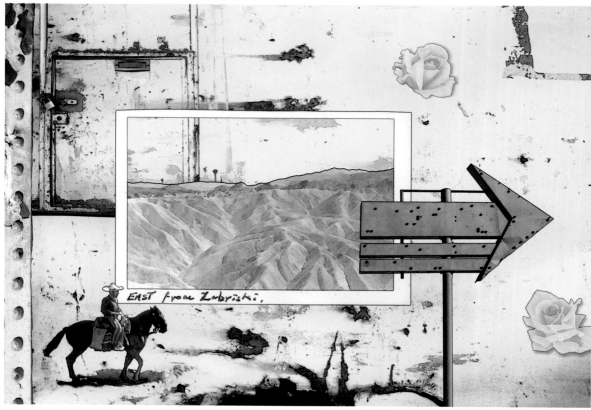

Nancy Tolford
California Street

self-promotion

Medium   **Digital**

Brief   **Personal work inspired by a trip to the U.S.A.**

Nancy Tolford
East from Zabriski

self-promotion

Medium   **Digital**

Brief   **Personal work inspired by a trip to the U.S.A.**

Simon Bartram
Sprouts Monsters

books

Medium   **Acrylic**

Brief   **Cover for a book of "Poems, pictures, doodles
                 and serious brain-thinking" titled "Watch Out For
                 Sprouts".**

Commissioned by **Mike Jolley**

Client   **Templar**

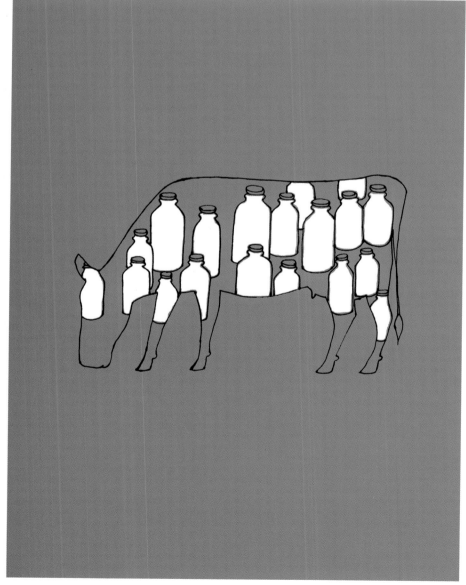

Alexandra Woods
Milkcow

self-promotion

Medium	Inkpen on paper then digitally modified
Brief	Response to self-researched and written text as follows 'THE AVERAGE DAIRY COW PRODUCES 11,500 PINTS OF MILK PER YEAR'.

Paul Bommer
La Campana (The Bell)

self-promotion

Medium	Digital
Brief	Monsters Loteria: The Monsters Illustration Collective's unique take on a traditional Mexican playing card game.

Paul Bommer
Train Robber

editorial

Medium	Digital
Brief	A piece about someone who broke into a school at night - just, it seems, to play with the kids' toys.
Commissioned by	Lawrence Bogle
Client	Times Educational Suppliment

Paul Bommer
Freudian Slips

self-promotion

Medium	Digital
Brief	Psychoanalytical underpants.

Paul Bommer
Loose Lips
editorial

Medium   Digital
Brief   Advice that a senior manager will do more harm
                than good if he shares with his staff information not
                meant for their ears.
Commissioned by Roger Browning
Client   The Guardian

127

1c. It's easy

1d. Fear of Knotweed

Andrew Baker
It's Easy

self-promotion

Medium	Drawing and digital
Brief	One of four linked images produced for the illustration exhibitions entitled SHED. Step 3: It's Easy.

Andrew Baker
Fear Of Knotweed

self-promotion

Medium	Drawing and digital
Brief	One of four linked images produced for the illustration exhibitions entitled SHED. Step 4: Fear of knotweed.

Andrew Baker
Human Hosts

editorial

Medium	Digital
Brief	For a Radio 4 programme about the many tiny species that call our bodies home.
Commissioned by	Jamie Trendall
Client	BBC Worldwide

Mike Ellis
Dorothy

self-promotion

Medium   Alkyd on canvas

Brief   Front cover vignette for 'The Wonderful Wizard
of Oz'.

Nishant Choksi
Early Grave?
editorial

Medium	**Digital**
Brief	**Avoid an early grave with a healthy work-life balance.**
Commissioned by	**Richard Krzyzak**
Client	**Property Week**

Nishant Choksi
The New Approach
editorial

Medium	**Digital**
Brief	**A radical shift in the way financial products are sold came into force on 1st June. Depolarisation means advisers can choose a new way of doing business.**
Commissioned by	**Justine Capelle**
Client	**Ft Business**

Nishant Choksi
Making Flexible Working Work
editorial

Medium	**Digital**
Brief	**Working outside the usual 9am to 5pm allows individuals to balance work with other responsibilities, including childcare.**
Commissioned by	**Marc Barker**
Client	**Caterer and Hotelkeeper**

Mark Hudson
The Dilemma
editorial

Medium　　　　　**Digital**
Brief　　　　　　**Choosing your pathway in life: Fulfilment or
dead-end?**
Commissioned by　**Steve Place**
Client　　　　　　**TSL Education**

133

Jonathan Gibbs
Hare & Tortoise

design

Medium	**Wood engraving**
Brief	**To illustrate 'persistence pays, winning slowly', showing Aesops fable, in relation to investment and the company's good results. For usage on brochure, cards and banners.**
Commissioned by	**Edward Hocknell**
Client	**Baillie Gifford**

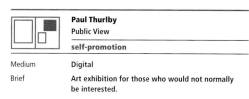

Paul Thurlby
Public View

self-promotion

Medium	Digital
Brief	Art exhibition for those who would not normally be interested.

135

Paul Thurlby
Sven & Rooney

self-promotion

Medium	Digital
Brief	Imagine the worst-case scenario for England leading up to the World Cup (this image was created prior to Rooney breaking his foot).

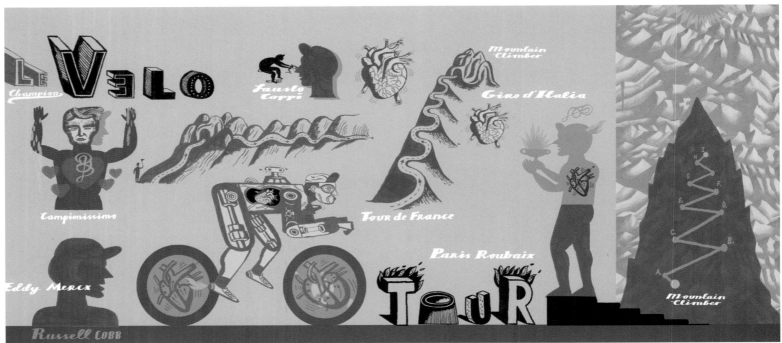

Russell Cobb
Xray

self-promotion

Medium	Ink
Brief	Book end for a book proposal called How it works. The image is taken from drawn elements on the subject of xray.

Russell Cobb
Le Velo Tour

self-promotion

Medium	Ink
Brief	Self promotion piece celebrating the sport of cycling.

Russell Cobb
Typo Landscape

self-promotion

Medium	Ink
Brief	Self promotion piece combining typography with Landscape.

Russell Cobb
Lateral Thinking
self-promotion

Medium	Ink
Brief	One of a series of self promotion pieces playing on the idea of innovation and lateral thinking.

 Russell Cobb
The Gardener

self-promotion

Medium   Ink

Brief   Image from an Illustrated story written by the artist,
        called The Gardener.

 Russell Cobb
Climate Change

self-promotion

Medium   Ink

Brief   Part of a proposal for a trip to Antarctica based on
        the theme of climate change.

Tom Denbigh
Raise Cash For Cafod

design

Medium | **Pen/ink and Photoshop**
Brief | **To produce a target poster for use in secondary schools to enable the charity to raise money for their causes.**
Commissioned by | **Cathy Hull**
Client | **Cafod**

Lara Harwood
Before Her Time

editorial

Medium	**Mixed medium**
Brief	Scientist have recently discovered what triggers puberty which they believe will help control when puberty happens and can prevent very young girls hitting puberty too young.
Commissioned by	**Alison Lawn**
Client	**New Scientist Magazine**

Lara Harwood
People At The Heart

design

Medium	**Watercolour and digital**
Brief	A generic illustration used in an in-house booklet for BDO on the Company's Brand, portaying company's core values ie in this case putting people at the heart of the business.
Commissioned by	**Lara Lockhart**
Client	**BDO Stoy Hayward**

Lara Harwood
Creative Thinking

editorial

Medium	**Mixed medium**
Brief	One of many illustrations on a feature in New Scientist about the processes of the creative mind.
Commissioned by	**Alison Lawn**
Client	**New Scientist Magazine**

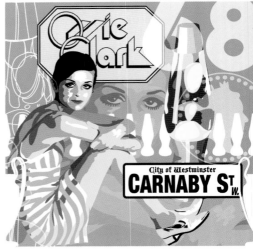

 Nick Reddyhoff
1968
_____
design

Medium	Computer generated
Brief	Illustrations of events, music, and TV from 1968.
Commissioned by	Conrad Davies
Client	Conrad Davies Design

 Michael Sheehy
Breaking Down Barriers
_____
self-promotion

| Medium | Mixed media |
| Brief | Christian and Muslim religious leaders are meeting in an attempt to break down barriers to understanding and cooperation. |

143

Simon Spilsbury
Whistlin' Mick

self-promotion

Medium   Lead/ink
Brief   Personal piece about American icons.

Simon Spilsbury
Mouse Surgery

self-promotion

Medium   Inks/paint
Brief   Part of an upcoming exhibition using Mickey
              Mouse as a conduit to illustrate idiosyncratic life in
              modern USA.

Simon Spilsbury
Drawn Porn

advertising

Medium   Pen/Photoshop
Brief   To draw 3000 sexual positions.
Commissioned by Menno Kluin, Alli Taylor
Client   Saatchi & Saatchi NY
Commissioned for Stuffit Expander

146

 Spiral Studio
Put Me On A Planet

design

Medium	**Photomontage/digital**
Brief	**The music is intelligent and quirky, this being a particularly upbeat outing for them. Listen to the CD & see what you come up with!**
Commissioned by	**Steve Cobby/Sim Lister**
Client	**23 Records**

 Caroline Tomlinson
Memoirs of a Geisha

self-promotion

Medium — Collage

Brief — To create an alternative book jacket design for Arthur Golden's novel 'Memoirs of a Geisha'.

 Caroline Tomlinson
The Almighty

self-promotion

Medium — Collage

Brief — For an article discussing why many women today are turning their back on religion and marriage.

Caroline Tomlinson
Grow

self-promotion

Medium — Collage

Brief — For an article discussing the pros and cons of using fertilizers in the garden to aid plant growth.

Rob White
I Love You Mr Lydon

editorial

Medium   Ink/pencil/digital

Brief   Article by musician Miles Hunt about John Lydon
             (Johnny Rotten) Sex Pistols musical influence on him
             and the defining moment when he first heard them.

Commissioned by   Jared Wilson (Editor)

Client   Leftlion.Co.Uk

Rob White
War 05

self-promotion

Medium   Ink/digital

Brief   Image usage purchased by Paul Smith Clothing from
             a selection or personal work based on the theme
             of War.

Commissioned by   Stuart Kirk

Client   Paul Smith/R Newbold

Josephine Sumner
Construction And Reflection

self-promotion

Medium   Scraperboard/digital

Brief   New Architecture by Tube, bus and river. To produce
             an artwork, suitable for use as a poster for TfL.

Client   Society Of Artists Agents / Transport For London

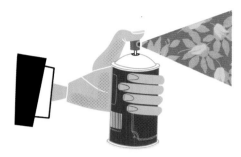

Ian Whadcock at Eastwing Agency
Space Solves

editorial

Medium	**Digital**
Brief	Letters page for DIY problems and household moves, re: design and decoration. Practical tips and specialist advice for consumers.
Commissioned by	**Bruno Harward**
Client	**The Guardian**

Ian Whadcock at Eastwing Agency
The Romance Of Proctology

editorial

Medium	**Digital**
Brief	Article looking at the bizarre combination of romance and Proctology in a famous §930's piece of research - part of the Improbable Research series in G2 Education.
Commissioned by	**John-Henry Barac**
Client	**The Guardian**

Ian Whadcock at Eastwing Agency
For Definite

editorial

Medium	**Digital**
Brief	A definite article on the definite article. Acknowledging "the" in index entries. Where do you put "the" in respect of a book's index?
Commissioned by	**John-Henry Barac**
Client	**The Guardian**

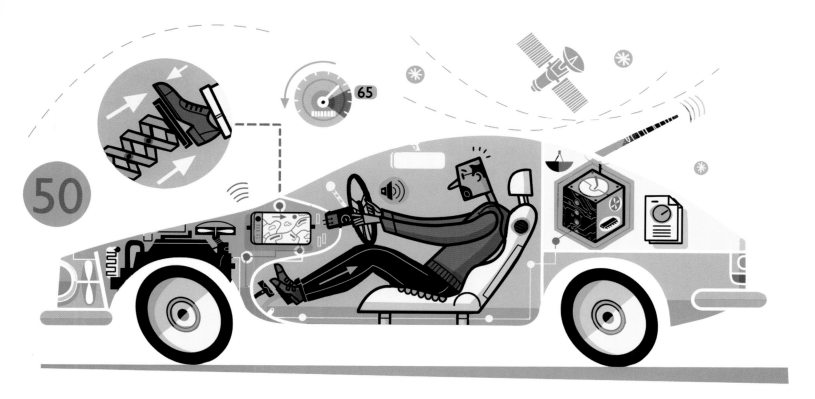

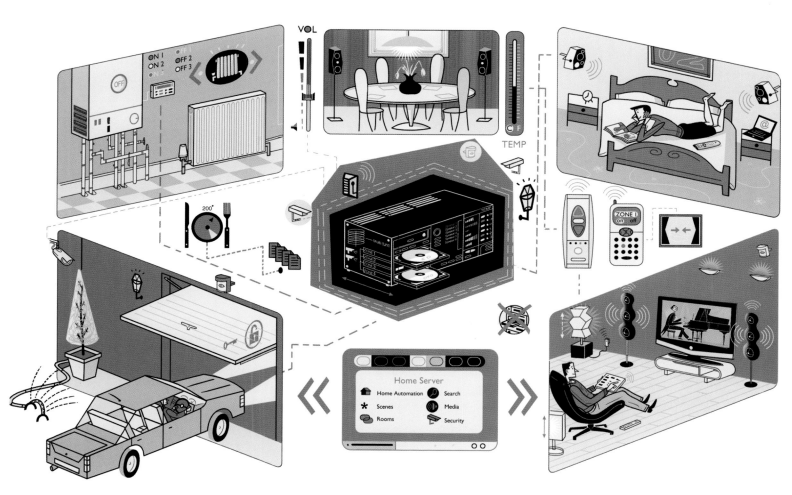

Ian Whadcock at Eastwing Agency
Coming Soon! Robocop In Your Car!

editorial

Medium	Digital
Brief	Intelligent technology could soon choose how fast and safely we all drive.
Commissioned by	Martin Colyer/Hugh Kyle
Client	Reader's Digest Magazine

Ian Whadcock at Eastwing Agency
All Wired Up

editorial

Medium	Digital
Brief	To illustrate how you plan and integrate new technology into a building project as it progresses towards completion.
Commissioned by	Kirsten Seymour/Mitch Davies
Client	Build-It Magazine

Stephen Collins
Swingers

editorial

Medium	Digital
Brief	Men's magazine piece about modern swingers' clubs.
Commissioned by	Helen Whitley-Niland
Client	GQ

Stephen Collins
The Queen

self-promotion

Medium	Digital
Brief	Self-promotional christmas card.
Commissioned by	Stephen Collins
Client	Stephen Collins Illustration

Sarah Dickie
Raspberry Leaf

self-promotion

Medium	Digital
Brief	To illustrate the health benefits of raspberry leaf tea for women.

Max Ellis
Airport Parking

editorial

Medium   **Digital**
Brief   **Make image to demonstrate the bad vibes of airport parking.**
Commissioned by   **Himesh Patel**
Client   **The Telegraph**

Max Ellis
All In The Game Note

advertising

Medium   **Digital**
Brief   **Create a bank note for a TV drama staring Ray Winstone. A wad was sent out in an envelope as a 'bung' to promotions companies.**
Commissioned by   **Ed Webster**
Client   **Channel 4 / 4 Creative**
Commissioned for   **Channel 4**

Chris Garbutt
Wireless Networking

editorial

Medium   **Digital**
Brief   **Illustration for an article on wireless technology for computers.**
Commissioned by   Andy Mcgregor
Client   **Future Publishing**

155

Harvey
Back In My Day

self-promotion

Medium	**Print / digital**
Brief	self promotion. 'Back in My Day'.

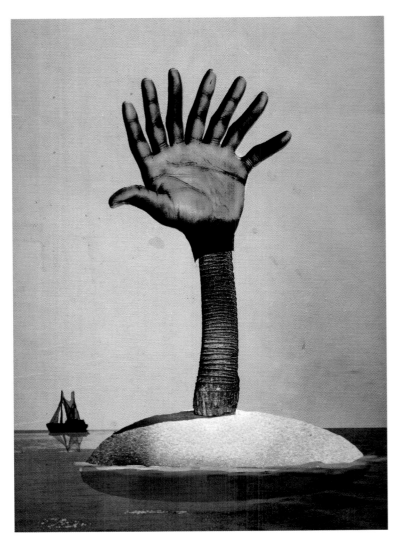

David Humphries
The Palm Tree
self-promotion

Medium   **Digital**
Brief   **To produce an iconic image of a palm tree - with a twist - for a Mexican lotteria game promotional mail out.**

David Humphries
Snakes and Ladders
self-promotion

Medium   **Digital**
Brief   **To visually display the vagaries of the stock market and investments.**

David Humphries
Bath
editorial

Medium   **Digital**
Brief   **The author fantasises about plotting naval battles in her bath.**
Commissioned by **Graham Black**
Client   **Financial Times**

157

David Humphries
Scotch Egg

editorial

Medium	Digital
Brief	The article described all things "Scotch Egg" and detailed the history of this unsung delicacy.
Commissioned by	Jocelyn Langer
Client	Delicious Magazine

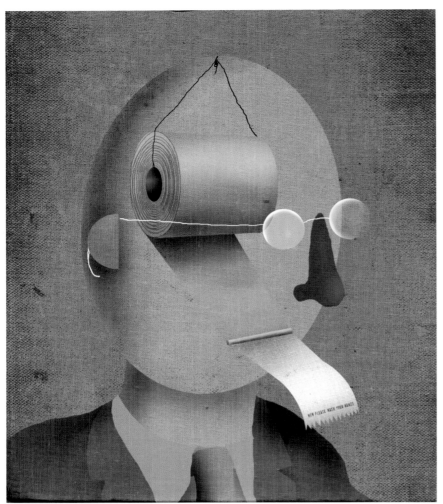

David Humphries

Yes Man

self-promotion

Medium   **Digital**

Brief   To depict a typical office creep for a self promotional
mail out.

David Humphries

Train Ticket Nightmares

editorial

Medium   **Digital**

Brief   Train companies are bullying passengers into paying
expensive penalty fares for being on the wrong
train- even though in many cases the mistake is
down to their own staff.

Commissioned by   **Martin Colyer/Hugh Kyle**

Client   **Reader'S Digest**

David Humphries

Louvre Pyramid

self-promotion

Medium   **Digital**

Brief   Part of a series of personal work on the subject of
art and science.

Bill Sanderson
St. Agnes

editorial

Medium	**Scraperboard and ink**
Brief	**To illustrate Keats atmospheric poem telling the story of the lovers Porphyrs and Madeleine.**
Commissioned by	**Jamie Trendall**
Client	**Radio Times**

159

Suzanne Barrett

DNA Figure

self-promotion

Medium   Acrylic

Brief   Illustration for a biography of Francis Crick,
co-discoverer of DNA - a figure to show how
certain characteristics and elements are determined
by DNA.

Paul Blow

Inheritance Tax

editorial

Medium   Digital

Brief   An article that looks at Inheritance Tax and how it
hits ordinary people.

Commissioned by   Martin Colyer/Hugh Kyle

Client   Reader's Digest

Paul Blow

Our Ken

editorial

Medium   Digital

Brief   To illustrate Simon Jenkins Friday column in the
Guardian - "Livingstone should guard his tongue but
not spare his language".

Commissioned by   Mike Topp

Client   Guardian Newspaper

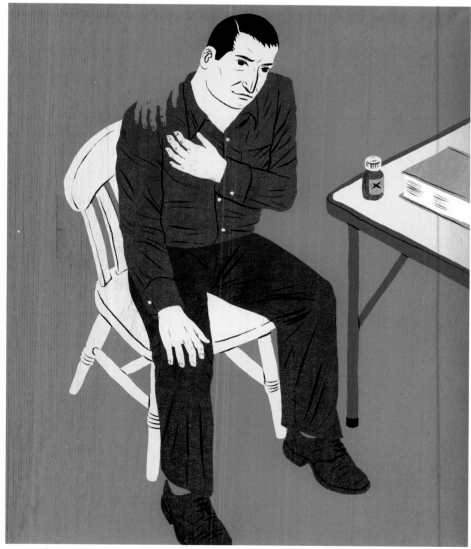

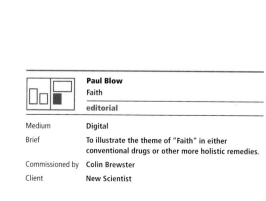

Paul Blow
Faith

editorial

Medium	**Digital**
Brief	**To illustrate the theme of "Faith" in either conventional drugs or other more holistic remedies.**
Commissioned by	**Colin Brewster**
Client	**New Scientist**

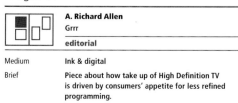

A. Richard Allen
Grrr

editorial

Medium	**Ink & digital**
Brief	**Piece about how take up of High Definition TV is driven by consumers' appetite for less refined programming.**
Commissioned by	**Carl Fleischer**
Client	**Future Publishing**

A. Richard Allen
Gallery Ennui
self-promotion

| Medium | Ink & digital |
| Brief | Personal piece based on a day spent in the National Gallery, observing occasionally very distrait-looking visitors and staff. |

A. Richard Allen
Chintz
self-promotion

| Medium | Ink, gouache, collage & digital |
| Brief | I intended to create an image using pattern rather than my usual flat colour. What started as a purely technical exercise produced unexpected narrative intrigue. |

Nick Hardcastle
The Police Spy
books

Medium	Pen and ink
Brief	To illustrate a scene from 'The Police Spy' by Joseph Conrad for 'The Spy's Bedside Book'.
Commissioned by	Joe Whitlock Blundell
Client	Folio Society

Nathan Daniels

Invite Only Internet

editorial

Medium	**Digital (freehand)**
Brief	**Areas of the internet now only available to an exclusive few by invite only.**
Commissioned by	**Carlton Hibbert**
Client	**Future Publishing**

Nathan Daniels

Free And Legal Mp3s

editorial

Medium	**Digital (freehand)**
Brief	**Where to find legally downloadable free mp3's (from record companies etc).**
Commissioned by	**Aston Leach**
Client	**Dennis Publishing**

Nathan Daniels

Then/Now Printing

editorial

Medium	**Digital (freehand)**
Brief	**How the digital revolution has streamlined the commercial print process.**
Commissioned by	**Simon Eastwood**
Client	**Haymarket**

165

 John Holcroft
Identity Theft

self-promotion

Medium   **Digital**

Brief   **People having their identities stolen so credit cards can be ordered and used in their name.**

 Laura Hughes
Rollerskates

self-promotion

Medium   Pencil/oils

Brief   Create images that convey a sense of the fast pace
and unpredictable nature of the wild west.

 Elly Walton
Axe To Grind

self-promotion

Medium   **Mixed**

Brief   self-promotional piece.

 Paul Boston
West Side Eateries

self-promotion

Medium   Digital

Brief   A detail from a 'stage set' of West Side Manhattan
that can be adapted to show various aspects of
day and night life. This picture celebrates the
idiosyncratic and cosmopolitan appetites of the
Big Apple.

Jan Bowman

Skateboarding In Lancaster Circus

books

Medium   **Digital**

Brief   **Illustration for *This Is Birmingham*, a picture book about aspects of the city that visitors usually miss.**

Jan Bowman

Shopping In Ladypool Road

books

Medium   **Digital**

Brief   **Illustration for *This Is Birmingham*, a picture book depicting aspects of the city that visitors usually miss.**

big man

Julian Crouch
Big Man

self-promotion

Medium | Digital woodcut
Brief | I was trying to capture the idea of the quintessential Glasgow hard man, the bonhomie, the menace and the stubborn dignity.

Julian Crouch
Theatre Crime No. 4

self-promotion

Medium | Digital woodcut
Brief | Part of a series of images made for a speculative theatrical site specific show in the Lightwell of Somerset House.

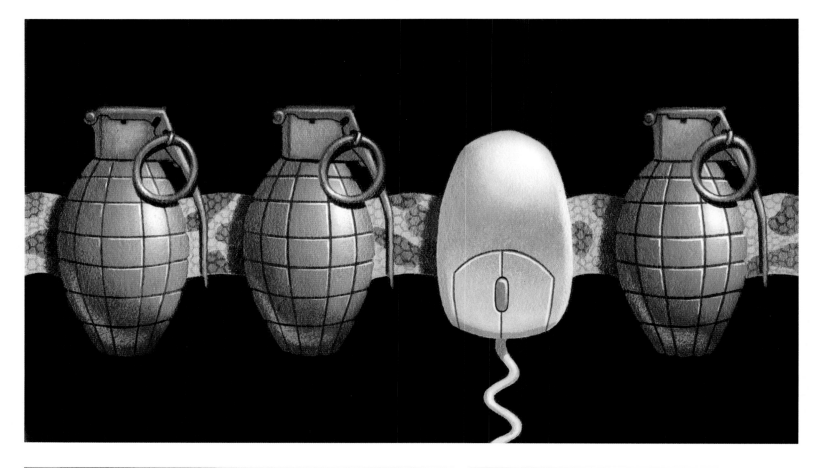

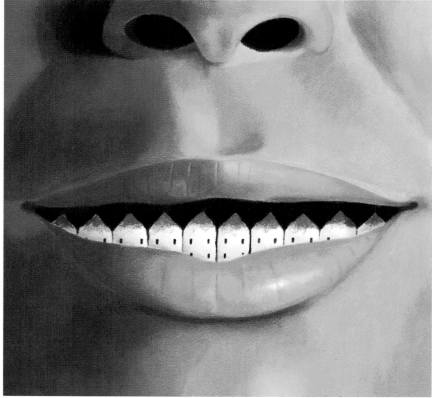

James Fryer
Cyber-Terrorism

editorial

Medium	Acrylic
Brief	To show how computers can be as deadly as weapons in terrorism.
Commissioned by	Martin Parfitt
Client	Future Publishing Ltd

James Fryer
Estate Agents

self-promotion

| Medium | Acrylic |
| Brief | To show the greed and hunger of estate agents chasing their commissions. |

James Fryer
James Fryer Illustration No.1

self-promotion

| Medium | Acrylic |
| Brief | The first in a series of adverts for James Fryer illustrator. All of the adverts will feature a red pencil within them. |

James Fryer
Blood On Their Hands

editorial

Medium	Acrylic
Brief	To show what a difficult job the EU commission has in deciding whether or not to let in countries with appalling war crimes records.
Commissioned by	Sara Wadsworth
Client	The Financial Times Ltd

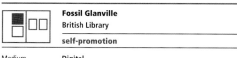

Fossil Glanville
British Library
self-promotion

| Medium | **Digital** |
| Brief | **Self-promotion: British Library.** |

tip 2:
boil the amount of water you need for
one cup of tea rather than a kettle full

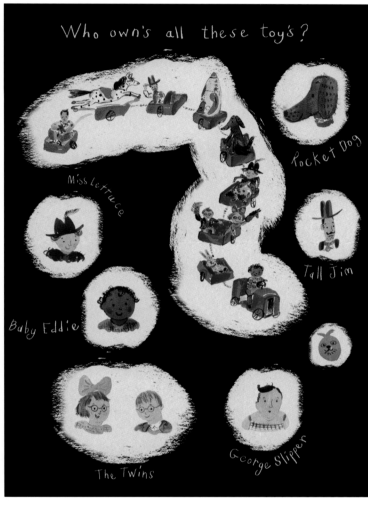

173

Fossil Glanville
How To Wear Clothes

editorial

Medium | Digital
Brief | For the column entitled 'How to Wear Clothes'. This issue was about summer dressing, "Blouses with buttons are more grown up than pull on t-shirts".
Commissioned by | Bruno Howard
Client | The Guardian

Fossil Glanville
Top Energy Saving Tips

self-promotion

Medium | Digital
Brief | Self-promotion: Energy Saving Tips.

Suzanna Hubbard
Toys

self-promotion

Medium | Mixed
Brief | To illustrate a wide and varied assortment of my own childrens book characters and their toys.

Andy Smith
A Lively Imagination

advertising

Medium	**Digital**
Brief	**Depict the line "a lively imagination can take you anywhere" with an image that is uplifting. Used for a recruitment poster for media law firm Olswang.**
Commissioned by	**Sarah Buttarazzi**
Client	**Columns Design**
Commissioned for	**Olswang**

Andy Smith
Me, Dead Dad and Alcatraz

books

Medium	**Digital**
Brief	**Create a colourful book jacket that also refers to the central characters' weight problem.**
Commissioned by	**Yeti McCaldin**
Client	**Bloomsbury**

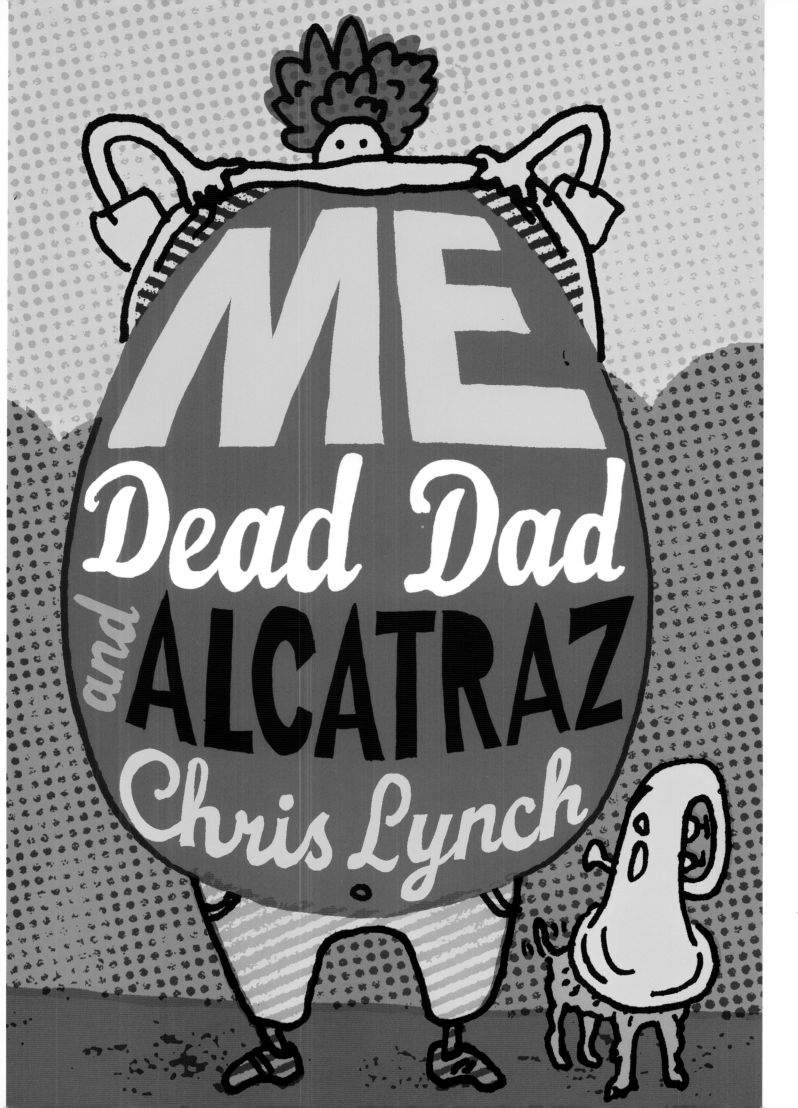

1934 - 2006

	Andy Smith
	Smash Martian
	advertising

Medium	**Digital**
Brief	**Create an image to be used as a memorial advertisement, for John Webster, the art director who created the Smash Martians.**
Commissioned by	**Sarah Thomson**
Client	**DDB London**
Commissioned for	**DDB London**

	Shane McG
	PHEW! Smudgy!
	books

Medium	**Digital**
Brief	**Single page spread in 32 page picture book about a boy who is horrified when he is given a tennis racquet for his birthday.**
Commissioned by	**Mike Jolley**
Client	**Templar**

	Shane McG
	Poor Ol' Spike Doesn't Play Tennis
	books

Medium	**Digital**
Brief	**Double page spread in 32 page picture book about a boy who is horrified when he is given a tennis racquet for his birthday.**
Commissioned by	**Mike Jolley**
Client	**Templar**

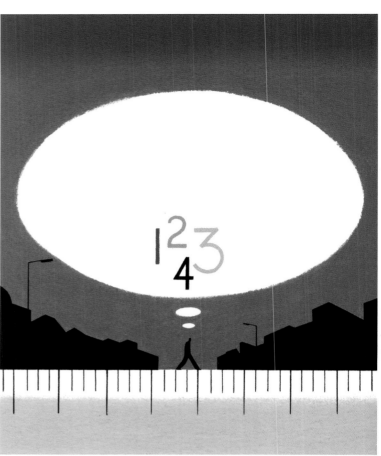

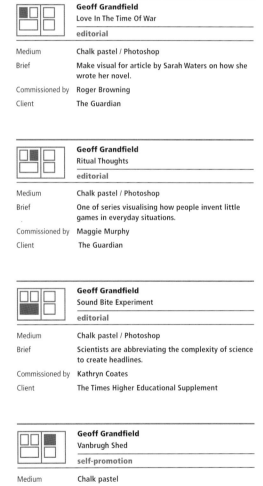

Geoff Grandfield
Love In The Time Of War

editorial

Medium	Chalk pastel / Photoshop
Brief	Make visual for article by Sarah Waters on how she wrote her novel.
Commissioned by	Roger Browning
Client	The Guardian

Geoff Grandfield
Ritual Thoughts

editorial

Medium	Chalk pastel / Photoshop
Brief	One of series visualising how people invent little games in everyday situations.
Commissioned by	Maggie Murphy
Client	The Guardian

Geoff Grandfield
Sound Bite Experiment

editorial

Medium	Chalk pastel / Photoshop
Brief	Scientists are abbreviating the complexity of science to create headlines.
Commissioned by	Kathryn Coates
Client	The Times Higher Educational Supplement

Geoff Grandfield
Vanbrugh Shed

self-promotion

Medium	Chalk pastel
Brief	Respond to a personal interpretation of the 'shed'.

179

Geoff Grandfield
The Lawless Roads

books

Medium	Chalk pastel / Photoshop
Brief	Read the novel by Graham Greene.
Commissioned by	Jasmine Lin
Client	Penguin (U.S.)

Rod Hunt
B-Movie City

self-promotion

Medium	Digital
Brief	Produce an image for a promotional A2 poster containing references to science fiction & fantasy movies. 21 movies are featured. Can you name them all?
Commissioned by	Rod Hunt

Rod Hunt
Change The World 9 To 5

books

Medium	Digital
Brief	Create a jacket image representing many different professions with the main cover folding out to a poster. Design all typography as part of the environment.
Commissioned by	Chris Wigan at Antidote
Client	We Are What We Do

Rod Hunt
1st Byte Headquarters

advertising

Medium	Digital
Brief	Produce a humorous representation of the 1st Byte headquarters, that shows the staff, workings & print equipment, for promotion advertising new digital print services.
Commissioned by	Lawrence Dalton
Client	1st Byte
Commissioned for	1st Byte

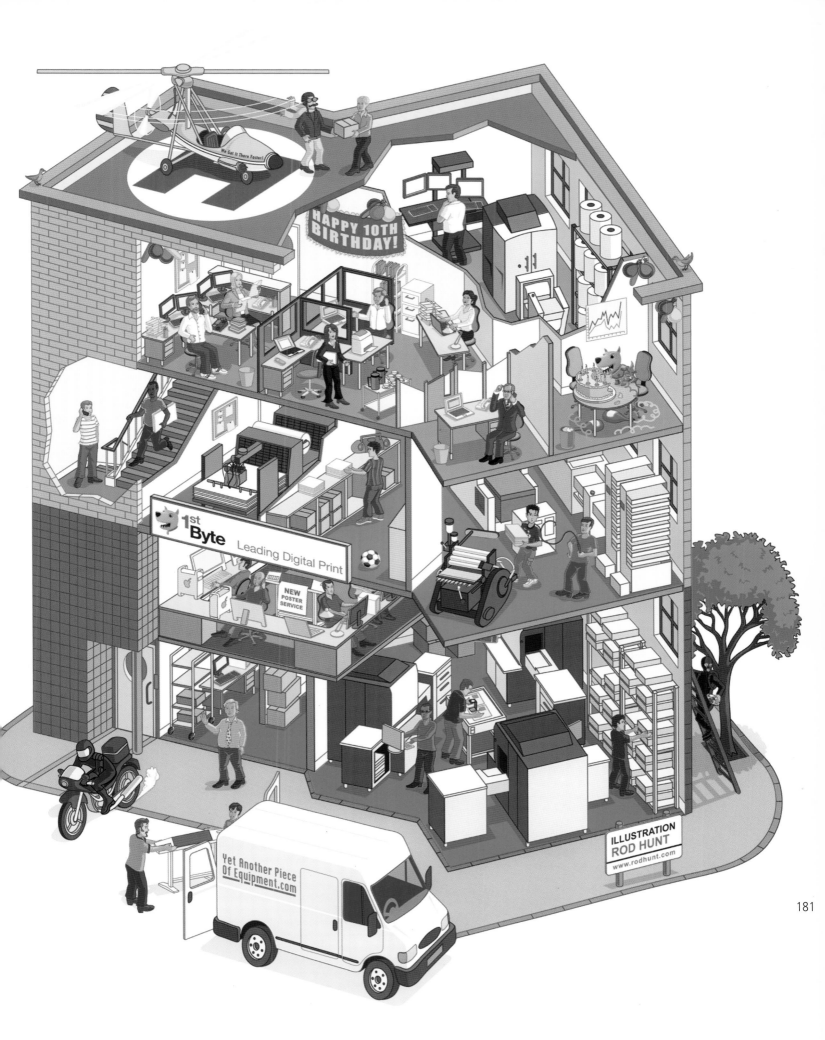

HAPPY 10TH BIRTHDAY!

1st Byte Leading Digital Print

NEW POSTER SERVICE

Yet Another Piece Of Equipment.com

We Get It There Faster!

Mandy Lindley
The Great Carrot Escape

self-promotion

Medium   Conté crayon

Brief   For a children's book I have written about carrots
            running away from a rabbit because they didn't
            want to be eaten.

Mandy Lindley
The Queen of the Night 01

self-promotion

Medium   Conté crayon

Brief   Mozart's "Magic Flute" opera. The evil queen of
            the night is portrayed as a cat dressed in sixteenth
            century French clothing.

Mandy Lindley
The Queen of the Night 02

self-promotion

Medium   Pencil

Brief   Mozart's "Magic Flute" opera. The evil queen of
            the night is portrayed as a cat dressed in sixteenth
            century French clothing.

Naomi Ryder
No Hoovering - More Kissing

self-promotion

Medium   Silkscreen with hand embroidery

Brief   Speculative/personal work on the subject of
                daydreaming whilst carrying out mundane day to
                day work.

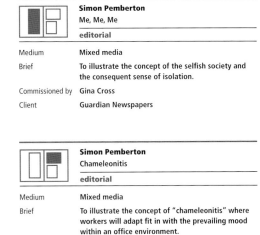

Simon Pemberton
Me, Me, Me

editorial

Medium	**Mixed media**
Brief	**To illustrate the concept of the selfish society and the consequent sense of isolation.**
Commissioned by	**Gina Cross**
Client	**Guardian Newspapers**

Simon Pemberton
Chameleonitis

editorial

Medium	**Mixed media**
Brief	**To illustrate the concept of "chameleonitis" where workers will adapt fit in with the prevailing mood within an office environment.**
Commissioned by	**Sarah Habershon**
Client	**Guardian Newspapers**

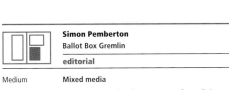

Simon Pemberton
Ballot Box Gremlin

editorial

Medium	**Mixed media**
Brief	**To illustrate the "malicious unseen forces" that were disappearing electoral ballots in a recent election.**
Commissioned by	**Gina Cross**
Client	**Guardian Newspapers**

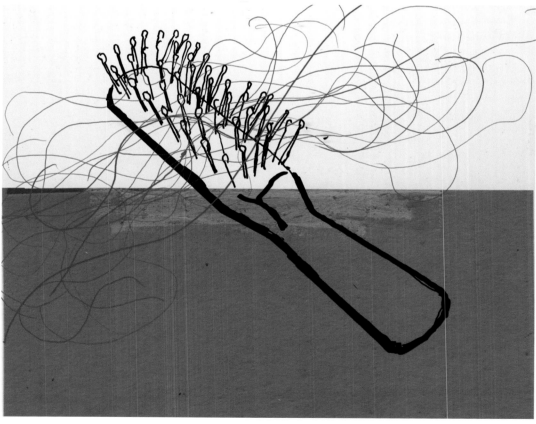

 Gary Sawyer
Ask Emma - Mascara

editorial

Medium	**Digital**
Brief	**ask emma - mascara.**
Commissioned by	**Pauline Doyle**
Client	**Guardian Newspapers**

 Gary Sawyer
Ask Emma - Hairloss

editorial

Medium	**Digital**
Brief	**ask emma - hairloss.**
Commissioned by	**Pauline Doyle**
Client	**Guardian Newspaper**

 Gary Sawyer
Poles Apart

editorial

Medium	**Digital**
Brief	**Concerns surrounding bipolar and the marketing of "mood stabilising" drugs to preschoolers.**
Commissioned by	**Craig Mackie**
Client	**New Scientist**

Lucille Toumi
Losing The Plot On House Prices

self-promotion

Medium   **Stitched textile collage**

Brief   Self initiated illustration produced in response to two major building societies giving house buyers conflicting information regarding the rise and fall of house prices.

Valentina Cavallini
Crows

self-promotion

Medium   Collage

Brief   Double page spread for a children's book.

Valentina Cavallini
Recycle It!

self-promotion

Medium   Photography

Brief   Poster promoting recycling.

Pete Brewster
Untitled

self-promotion

Medium   Scraperboard

Brief   Self-initiated piece.

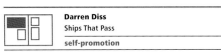

	Darren Diss
	Ships That Pass
	self-promotion
Medium	Mixed
Brief	'Ships that Pass' is an illustration to accompany an article exploring human tendencies to invent 'systems to live by'. In this case the financial infrastructure of currency markets.

	Darren Diss
	Kiss On The Lips
	self-promotion
Medium	Mixed
Brief	Kiss on the Lips was produced as part of a series based on emoticons. In this case :-X

	Anna - Louise Felstead MA (RCA)
	The Ivy Kitchen
	self-promotion
Medium	Ink on paper
Brief	Part of a series from my 'Glamorous London Restaurants' exhibition, held in September 2006.

	Anna - Louise Felstead MA (RCA)
	View From Flyco
	advertising
Medium	Ink & pastel on paper
Brief	The Royal Navy commissioned me to produce illustrations on board HMS Illustrious for their promotional literature.
Commissioned by	Captain Brian Warren
Client	The Royal Navy
Commissioned for	Royal Navy

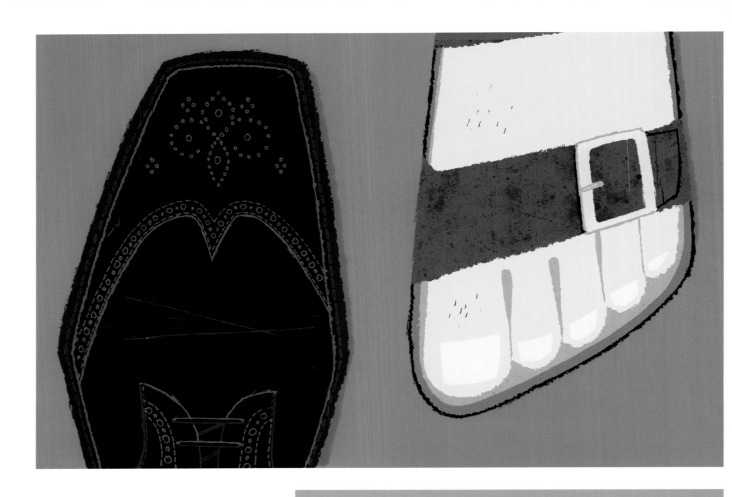

Adrian Johnson
Shoo-In

editorial

Medium	Digital
Brief	Housing associations and city investors are cosying up in the social housing sector.
Commissioned by	Richard Krzyzak
Client	Property Week

Peter Grundy
Hampton Court Eating

books

Medium	Adobe Illustrator
Brief	Create a diagram to show how much food was eaten in the court of Henry 8 at Hampton Court.
Commissioned by	Zoë Bather
Client	Wolf Olins

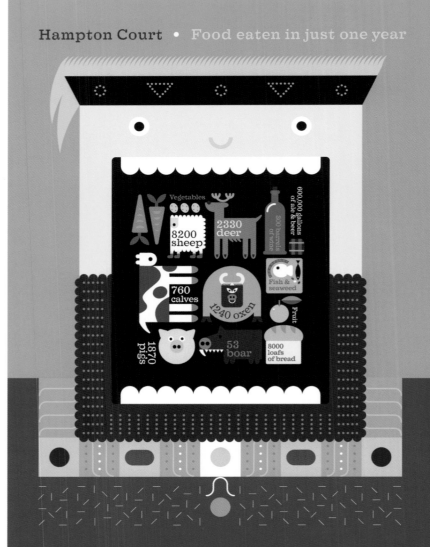

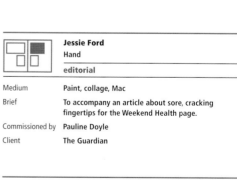

Jessie Ford
Hand

editorial

Medium	Paint, collage, Mac
Brief	To accompany an article about sore, cracking fingertips for the Weekend Health page.
Commissioned by	Pauline Doyle
Client	The Guardian

Jessie Ford
Boat

design

Medium	Paint, collage, Mac
Brief	To create a cover for the 2006 Aldeburgh Poetry Festival. To include the traditional theme of a boat.
Commissioned by	Naomi Jaffa
Client	The Poetry Trust

PENGUIN ( ) CLASSICS

Sir Gawain and the Green Knight

Translated by BERNARD O'DONOGHUE

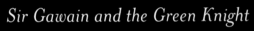

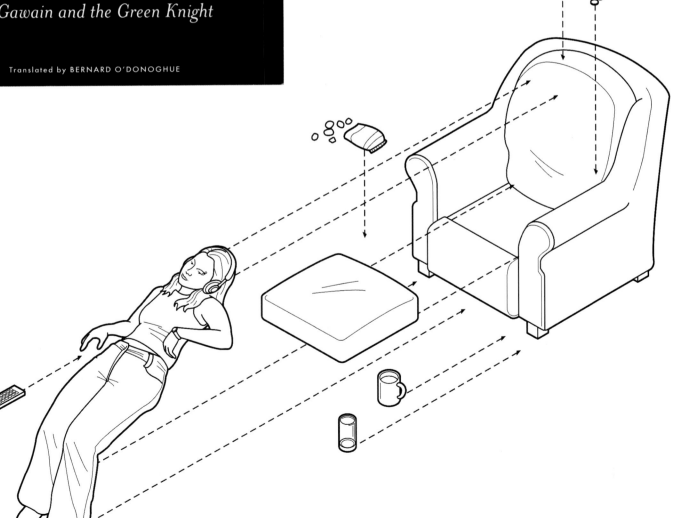

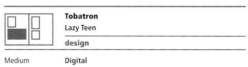

Swava Harasymowicz
Sir Gawain And The Green Knight

books

Medium	Mixed
Brief	A cover for Penguin Classics 2006 edition of Sir Gawain and the Green Knight, translated by Bernard O'Donoghue.
Commissioned by	Samantha Johnson
Client	Penguin Books

Tobatron
Lazy Teen

design

Medium	Digital
Brief	Appropriating the visual language of an instructional diagram or air-fix kit, show how an Electrolux hoover can clean round even the laziest of teenagers.
Commissioned by	Gary Wallis
Client	Lowe Worldwide

Purdi Gibson
A Walk In The Park

advertising

Medium	Collage
Brief	Poster image used in-store and in publications to promote a range of vitamins to ease hayfever symptoms in Australia.
Commissioned by	Mark Carlson
Client	Carlson Health
Commissioned for	Microgenics Vitamins

195

Purdi Gibson
The Last Supper

self-promotion

Medium	Acrylic on textured board
Brief	An illustrative review of the 90's black comedy movie, "The Last Supper". Staring Cameron Diaz and Courtney B Vance.

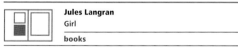

Jules Langran
Fall

books

Medium	Digital
Brief	One of four images commissioned for the Die-Gestalten 'Spooky' calendar.
Commissioned by	Die Gestalten Verlag
Client	Die Gestalten Verlag

Jules Langran
Girl

books

Medium	Digital
Brief	One of four images commissioned for the Die-Gestalten 'Spooky' calendar.
Commissioned by	Die Gestalten Verlag
Client	Die Gestalten Verlag

Jules Langran
Wave

books

Medium	Digital
Brief	One of seven images commissioned for Die-Gestalten 1001 Nights.
Commissioned by	Die Gestalten Verlag
Client	Die Gestalten Verlag

Henning Löhlein
Cheeky Dog Doesn't Have Any Time Anymore

books

Medium	Acrylic
Brief	Cheeky Dog, after having puppies she didn't have time to be cheeky anymore.
Commissioned by	IR Paxman
Client	AltBerliner

Henning Löhlein
Small Fish In The Big Sea

books

Medium	Acrylics
Brief	A gift book about a penguin trying to find his luck (the big sea is not where it will be found).
Commissioned by	Bärbel Brand
Client	Sanssouci

Steve May
Cinderella

books

Medium	Digital
Brief	Cover Illustration for a "Play Along" Cinderella Book, including an interactive CD Rom.
Commissioned by	Keren Greenfield
Client	Harper Collins

199

Alice Potterton
Joking Apart

books

Medium	Ink and digital
Brief	My third collection of poetry titled 'Joking apart' has been accepted for publication by The Collective Press. Could you produce an illustration for the cover?
Commissioned by	Alicia Stubbersfield
Client	The Collective Press

Peter Hutchinson

A Rolling Stone Gathers Some Moss?

self-promotion

Medium	Pen and ink on newsprint
Brief	Image of this long-standing band member of the Rolling Stones - maybe some cracks are showing from years of playing too hard?

Peter Hutchinson

Lady Madonna

self-promotion

Medium	Pen and ink on newsprint
Brief	Image tries to get under the skin of this modern icon by manipulating the photo and dissecting her limb by limb - how strange?

sheet one
sketchs
N. England
&
London
summer 2005.

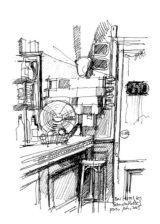

sheet two
sketchs
N. France
&
Paris
summer 2005.

Peter Hutchinson
So, What Did You Do Last Summer?

self-promotion

Medium   Pen and ink into sketchbook

Brief   I carry a sketchbook with me to record visually my travel experiences - last summer's trip to England and France was no exception - fond memories.

Linda Hughes
Walthamstow-On-Sea

self-promotion

Medium	**Digitally coloured drawings**
Brief	**An updated version of William Morris'** **"News from Nowhere", imagining Walthamstow's** **urban landscape 100 years in the future, as a** **seaside resort.**

Linda Hughes
The Bell Corner

self-promotion

Medium	**Digitally coloured drawing**
Brief	**An updated version of William Morris'** **"News from Nowhere", imagining Walthamstow's** **urban landscape 100 years in the future, as a** **seaside resort.**

Sarah Gibb
Annie May's Black Book

books

Brief	**To produce cover artwork.**
Commissioned by	**Jeremy Butcher**
Client	**Simon & Schuster**

Annie May's
Black Book

debby holt

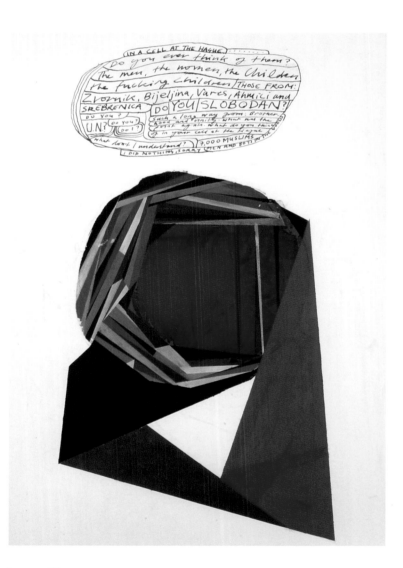

Paul Bowman

Milosevic At The Hague

self-promotion

Medium	Acrylic, pen and ink on paper
Brief	Personal reflection on Slobodan Milosevic's thoughts at the Hague, imprisoned for war crimes. Did he think about the death and destruction caused by his actions?

Angela Hogg

The Book Of Story Beginnings

books

Medium	Mixed
Brief	To produce a book jacket for a children's novel about a boys adventure in a land ruled by cats and birds.
Commissioned by	Jim Bunker
Client	Walker Books

Helen Wakefield

Sudoku

editorial

Medium	Digital
Brief	To illustrate a Sudoku Puzzle Page in a free manner, with a Japanese influence.
Commissioned by	Martin Colyer/Hugh Kyle
Client	Reader's Digest

Kevin Ward

Word Up Weirdo

self-promotion

Medium	Ink, acrylic, paper, Photoshop
Brief	Speculative flyer design for literary events featuring unknown writers. Starting with smudged fingerprints, I wanted to capture a sense of live presence, grit and humour.

Brian Grimwood
Flamenco
advertising

Medium	**Paint and brush**
Brief	**Wine label and poster image.**
Client	**HKA design**

Brian Grimwood
Death's Echo

books

Medium	Pen & ink, computer
Brief	Illustrating A W.H. Auden poem.
Client	Folio Society

Andrew MacGregor
Corporate Slum

self-promotion

Medium	Acryllic, Pen, pencil, digital
Brief	What is a slum? Corporate 'Fatcats' living in a squalid bubble of self-importance, sleaze and corruption.

Choose the Science,
Get the Magic.

Hair Room
Applause

(C) Ayako Morisawa

Adria Meserve

Marry A Princess!

books

Medium	Acrylic, gouache, digital
Brief	This is one of the full colour illustrations for the picture book 'The Mermaid, the Prince and the Happy Ever After'. The King is attempting to persuade a reluctant Prince Bernard to marry for money so they can repair their leaky castle.
Commissioned by	Louise Bolongaro

Ayako Morisawa

Applause

advertising

Medium	Collage with acrylic gouache, paper, fabric, string and Photograph.
Brief	This is a poster for a hair Salon called Applause. I've created this image with natural colours to suit the salon's atmosphere.
Commissioned by	Koji Sato
Client	Hair Room Applause
Commissioned for	Poster

Bob Venables

Profit Hunter

advertising

Medium	Acrylic
Brief	One of a series of illustrations for Artemis Financial Group, about the length they go to when hunting profits.
Commissioned by	Russel Wailes
Client	RPM3

209

Mark Thomas

Christmas Cover

editorial

Medium	Acrylic inks and goache
Brief	To create the Christmas cover for the Radio Times encompassing Christmas and the top rated show Doctor Who.
Commissioned by	Shem Law
Client	Radio Times

Benedict Siddle
Manhattan May Day Midnight
self-promotion

Medium	Screenprint
Brief	Illustrate the poem "Manhattan May Day Midnight" by Allen Ginsberg.

Dominic Trevett
Pitch For Morphy Richards
self-promotion

Medium	Pen and ink
Brief	Make notes on the humble toaster.

Jackie Parsons
Secret London
editorial

Medium	Mixed
Brief	To illustrate an article about hidden or secret spots of tranquility in London.
Commissioned by	Richard Keenan
Client	Time Out

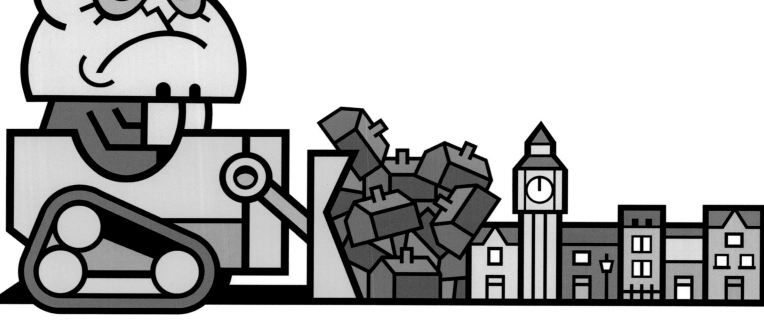

 Maria Raymondsdotter
New Lanes

advertising

Medium	**Pen & ink + Photoshop**
Brief	**Illustration for a brochure and outdoor sign informing of new cycle lanes in a part of Stockholm.**
Commissioned by	**Mia Lifsten**
Client	**Formia**
Commissioned for	**Stockholms Gatukontor**

 Matt Pattinson
Bulldozer

editorial

Medium	**Digital**
Brief	**The treasury is trying to push through housing on green belt land.**
Commissioned by	**Richard Krzyzak**
Client	**Property Week**

Sara Nunan
Streetwise Feature: Connaught Village

advertising

Medium	**Pen and watercolour**
Brief	**A map of this area of London showing shop fronts that pay the magazine "Grove" for advertising/ editorial.**
Commissioned by	**Lucy Cleland and Apara Maney**
Client	**Archant/Metropolis Publishing**

Brett Ryder
Key To The City

editorial

Medium	**Digital**
Brief	A key to the regeneration of cities lies in the integration of key services.
Commissioned by	**Rob Howells**
Client	**Property Week**

Billy Seabrook
A Forest

advertising

Medium	**Mixed media**
Brief	An image used as part of the Autumn/Winter 2006 Brooklyn Seasonal Fashion Collection.
Commissioned by	**Patrick Meaney**
Client	**Brooklyn Bow & Ribbon Ltd**
Commissioned for	**2006 Collection**

Dandi Palmer
Cover For Great Oak, Little Acorns

books

Medium	**Line and watercolour**
Brief	Cover and illustrations for the life cycle of an oak tree. Suitable for 3 to 7 year olds. Picture book format.
Client	**Wings Plants and Paws**

215

Patrick Regout
Dating Guide

editorial

Medium	Pen & ink and digital colours
Brief	For a Guardian Weekend copy about "dating guides" and why people read these self-help books.
Commissioned by	Maggie Murphy
Client	Guardian Newspapers Ltd.

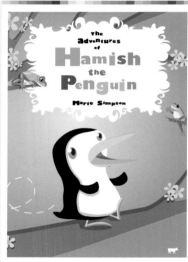

Orly Orbach

Bunny Club

editorial

Medium   **Ink on paper**

Brief   (illustration for a short story) A man encounters a
            woman in the tube, which he stood up on a date
            because of her rabbit like featurers.

Commissioned by   **Martin Bax**

Marie Simpson

Hamish and Friends

self-promotion

Medium   **Digital**

Brief   A poster aimed at children and book buyers to
            promote my work. Designed to be folded in 4 and
            posted out for the propose of advertising.

Sue Mason

Fame Joins The Ocd Clinic

books

Medium   **Digital**

Brief   Comparison of how the general public's
            infatuation with fame is akin to an obsessional
            compulsive disorder.

Commissioned by   **Matthew Newton**

Client   www.poison-control.com

Fame joins the OCD clinic

217

 Thea Brine
Modern Poverty

editorial

Medium   Mixed media

Brief   Poor young men are often designer label
                obsessed, they strive and steal to wear the right
                clothes but this often ends up with a trip to the
                local youth court.

Commissioned by John Henry Barac

Client   The Guardian

Neil Shrubb

Silver Shoppers

editorial

Medium	Digital
Brief	The elderly are set to become the major spending force in the near future.
Commissioned by	Richard Krzyzak
Client	Property Week

Lucie Sheridan

Geisha

self-promotion

Medium	Pen and ink/Photoshop

Lucy MacLeod

British Airways

advertising

Medium	Mixed medium
Brief	To communicate the concept of 10 flights a day to New York.
Commissioned by	Kate Blumer
Client	BBH
Commissioned for	British Airways

London to New York. 10 times a day.

BRITISH AIRWAYS

 **Hannah McVicar**
Garden Furniture

books

Medium	**Screenprint**
Brief	**To create a full page illustration for 'The Little Book of Quick Fixes for the Impatient Gardener' by Gay Search, to begin the chapter on garden furniture.**
Commissioned by	**Helen Lewis**
Client	**Quadrille Publishing**

 Christopher Halsall
The Power of Reading

self-promotion

Medium	**Mixed media**
Brief	**To produce an image that illustrates the endless imaginative possibilities inspired by reading.**

 Christopher Halsall
Enveloped by City Life

self-promotion

Medium   **Mixed media**

Brief   **To produce a satirical image depicting an individual's capitulation to city life and its ideals.**

Stephen Hall
UK Jam

self-promotion

Medium	Digital
Brief	Motorway congestion in the UK is on the increase, but all that motorists can do is pray it doesn't happen to them.

a crashing
sound -
coming from
the kitchen

who's that then?

that's the
little gardeners

Øivind Hovland
Peeking

books

Medium   Drawing/Photoshop
Brief   Images part of my children's book 'The Little People
          - Introducing the little Gardeners'

Øivind Hovland
Who's That Then?

books

Medium   Drawing/Photoshop
Brief   Images part of my children's book 'The Little People
          - Introducing the little Gardeners'.

Tim Marrs
Split Images

books

Medium	Digital
Brief	One of a series of images for the re-branding and publication of Elmore Leonard's back catologue.
Commissioned by	Mark Ecob
Client	Orion / Phoenix Paperbacks

David Bromley
Mullamuddy Creek

self-promotion

Medium	Mixed media
Brief	Self promotion image combining a linocut of a scene near Mudgee NSW Australia and digital.

Jo Halstead
Cuba!

self-promotion

Medium	Acrylic, ink, collage and Photoshop
Brief	An illustration for a 'Traveller's Tales' book to highlight a traveller's experience of a particular destination, in this case Cuba.

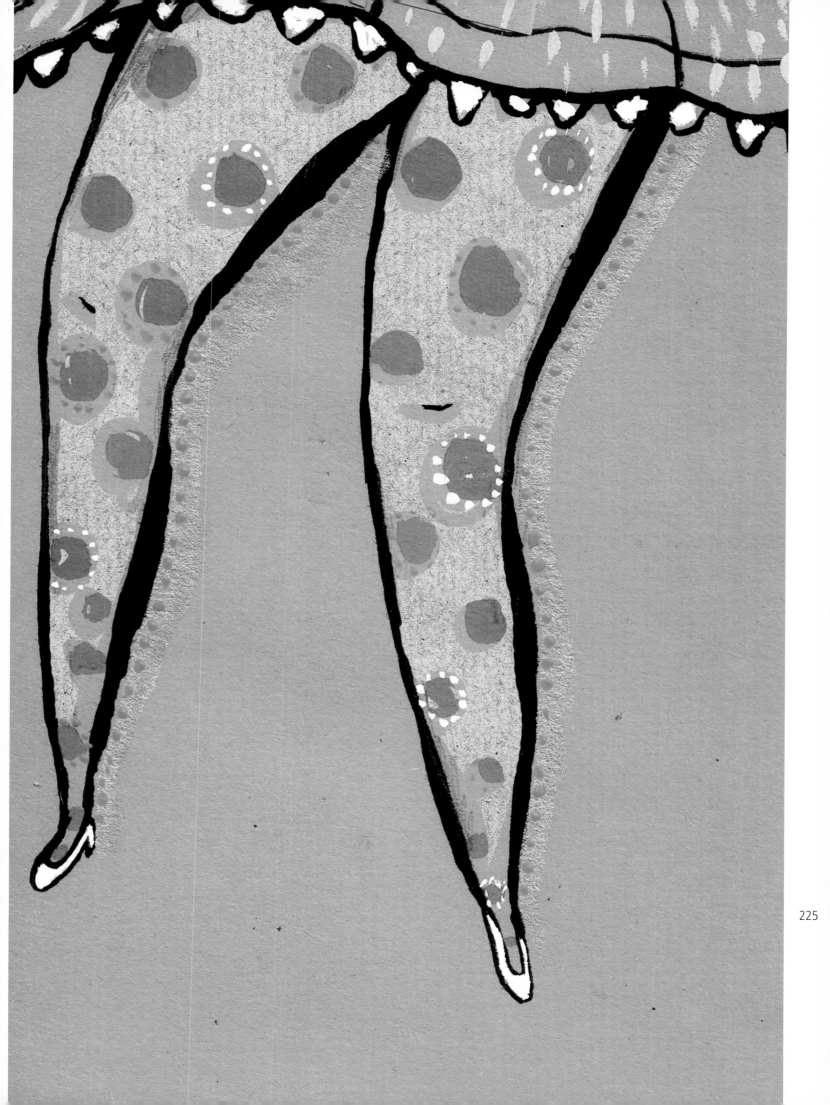

 Louise Weir
Are Animals Too Cocky

editorial

Medium	Acrylic
Brief	To Illustrate a piece showing animals that cause havoc around the world. Highlighting monkeys in India that steal food and money from office workers that are powerless to act against them because they are holy animals.
Commissioned by	Declan Fahey
Client	Dennis publishing

Louise Weir
Sienna Miller Portrait

editorial

Medium	Acrylic
Brief	To produce a portrait of Sienna Miller in an exotic setting that looks glamorous and inviting for the Summer cover.
Commissioned by	Ian Pendleton
Client	Showmedia

Oliver Harud
Tea Drinker

self-promotion

Medium   **Digital**

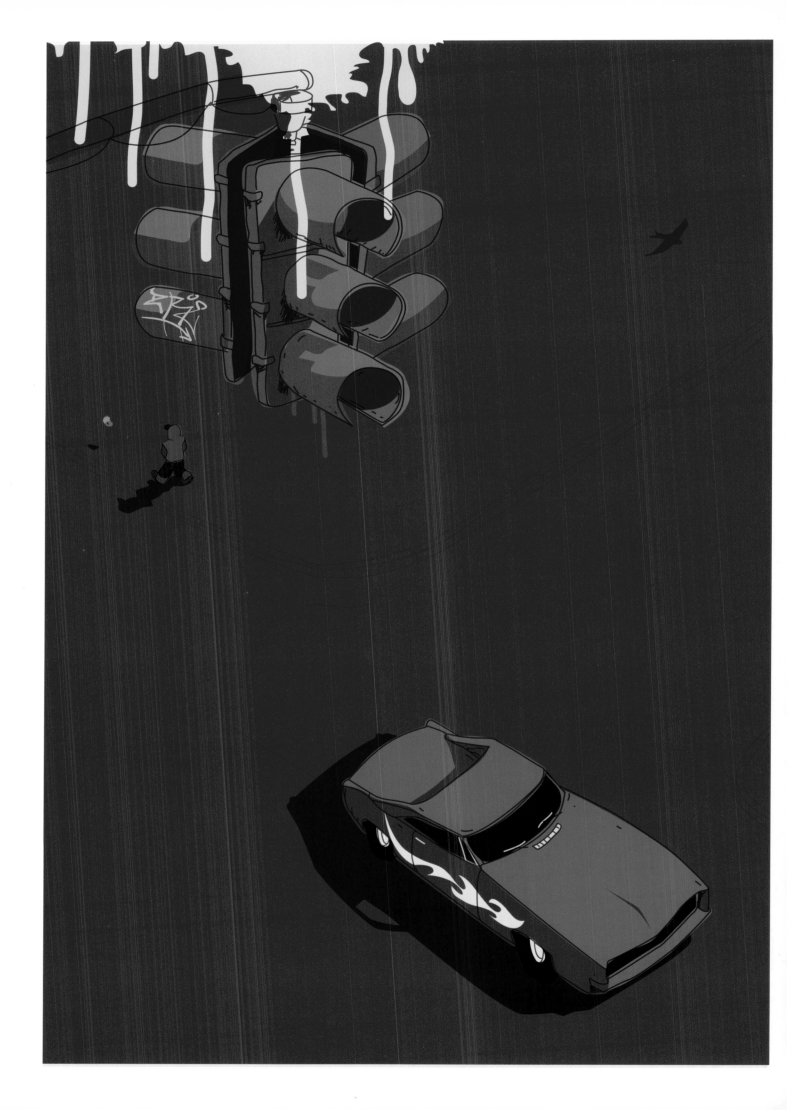

Peter Mac

Drive It Like You Stole It

self-promotion

| Medium | Digital |
| Brief | Self promotion piece to illustrate the words 'drive it like you stole it' It just came to me in a dream!!! |

Peter Mac

Name Dropping

editorial

Medium	Digital
Brief	To illustrate an article about the proliferation of supermarkets selling insurance.
Commissioned by	Henry Redman
Client	Cedar Communications

Charlie Sutcliffe

Untitled

books

Medium	Ink, paper, Photoshop
Brief	To create a visual narrative to discribe a Doppelgaenger Metropolis.
Commissioned by	David Lynch
Client	Izumi Records

Charlie Sutcliffe

Untitled

books

Medium	Ink, paper, Photoshop
Brief	To describe a visual narrative within a Doppelgaenger Metropolis.
Commissioned by	David Lynch
Client	Izumi Records

Fine-n-Dandy

The Neopolitan Tryptich

self-promotion

Medium	Screenprint
Brief	A series of posters celebrating traditions & customs of bank holidays.

1

2

3

4

5

New Talent

Judges

Karen Bird [1]
Designer/Director, Peloton Design

Karen graduated in 1994 and worked in London for five years with a number of agencies. 3 years of those were spent at Addison Design.

She moved to Bristol in 1999, worked at local agencies and was a part-time lecturer at Bath Spa University on the BA graphic design course. In 2004, she joined partnerships with Peter Thompson to form Peloton Design. Clients include Herman Miller, the University of Bristol and The Tour of Britain.

www.pelotondesign.co.uk

"It has been encouraging to see a strong and diverse depth of talent from the students. We just need more clients who are willing to appreciate the works, too."

Lucy Scherer [2]
Director, The Artworks

Lucy Scherer studied modern languages at Oxford University and trained as a solicitor for 2 years, after which she was unsurprisingly keen to move into a more creative field, and so worked first for literary agents Peters Fraser & Dunlop before covering maternity leave at The Artworks illustration agency in 1999. That led to stints at 2 other illustration agents, Arena and Black & White Line, before she returned to The Artworks in 2002. She now runs the agency with her colleague Stephanie Alexander.

"The judging process was very easy to navigate and it was encouraging to find some interesting new talent among the student submissions, hopefully the bright stars of the future."

James Sommerville [3]
Co-Founder and Group Creative Director, ATTIK

James Sommerville studied graphic design at Batley School of Art before co-founding ATTIK (1986) with partner Simon Needham. Today, he has a Group Creative Director role working with key clients in Europe, Asia and USA. He devised ATTIK's UK MA course and is personal adviser to The Prince's Trust. ATTIK are the longest serving Trust from 60,000 start-up businesses in 30 years. He is also Co-Creative Editor of Noise books with partner Simon.

James Stevens [4]
Deputy Creative Director, HarperCollins

James Stevens studied at University of Central Lancashire. He worked for a small design company in Colchester before joining HarperCollins Children's Books, where he has been for the last 7 years.

He has designed award-winning books with such talented illustrators as Oliver Jeffers, Russell Ayto and Emma Chichester Clark.

"The high standard on show made judging very hard but also a pleasure."

Matthew Richardson [5]
Illustrator

Matthew Richardson was born and brought up in London. He studied Graphic Design at Middlesex Polytechnic, followed by postgraduate study in Illustration at Central St Martins. He recently completed an MA in Fine Art at UWIC (Cardiff).

He has worked for many and varied clients including the London Sinfonietta, Random House, Carling, Yellowhammer, Channel 4 TV, Penguin Books, Hodder Books, Radio Times, Quartet Books, The British Council, HarperCollins Books, The Guardian, Macmillan Books, The Sunday Times, World of Interiors, BT, Decca, EMI, WPP and New Scientist.

Alongside working to commission, Matthew also pursues and exhibits his own work, which utilises a diverse range of processes such as print, photography, drawing, the moving image, assemblage and various digital media.

"Judging the student entries was a tricky but highly enjoyable experience. It is becoming increasingly hard to make work that is visible in our image-saturated world. So now, more than ever, those images which are genuinely original tend to shine out. I know we have found some real shiners here."

GOLD

Michael Kirkham

The Short Happy Life Of Francis Macomber

Ednburgh College of Art

Medium	**Acrylic**
Brief	**To illustrate Hemingway's "The Short Happy Life of Francis Macomber".**
Course Leader	**Jonathan Gibbs**
Course	**Illustration**
Head of Department	**Jonathan Gibbs**

Michael was born in Birmingham but spent a greater proportion of growing up time in Harrogate, N Yorks. He is unusually lucky in all respects except for a tendency to receive blows to the head. He completed and thoroughly enjoyed Foundation studies at the admirable (although somewhat bleak) Harrogate College.

Michael was recently wrenched from the womb-like comfort of Edinburgh College of Art's excellent illustration department and cast mercilessly into real life.

He moved to London with a beautiful girlfriend to look after a temporarily abandoned house and a temporarily abandoned cat. In 2006, he won a D&AD Best New Blood award.

Michael spent the summer after graduating with:

- riding trains around central London with naught but a portfolio for company,

- working as illustrator for Random House and Televisual Magazine,

- deviously constructing self promotional material, - posting the aforementioned material into the ether,

- checking email at five minute intervals for response from aforementioned ether.

During office hours, Michael can be found hunched at desk drawing straight-faced people and bare limbed trees (except between the hours of 1pm and 2pm when he can be found in kitchen watching 'The World At War' and eating lunch).

He is currently working on a short film entitled "Sometimes in the Night Time" and anticipating a blow to the head of unprecedented severity to counterbalance recent wave of incredible good fortune.

1 Sketches
2 Winning illustration

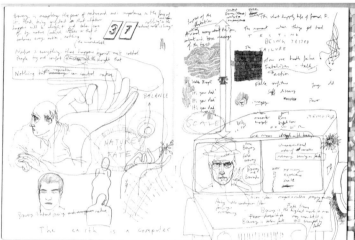

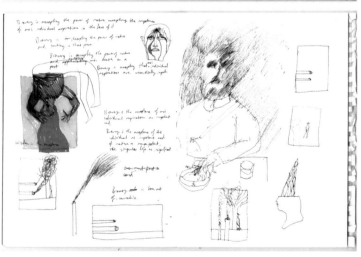

SILVER

David Callow
Conflict Diamonds

Arts Institute of Bournemouth

Medium	**Digital collage**
Brief	**A set of decorative/commenting/informing illustrations for an article on the diamond mining issues of Angola and Sierra Leone.**
Course Leader	**Amanda Evans**
Course	**BA (Hons) Illustration**
Head of Department	**Amanda Evans**

Graduating from the Arts Institute at Bournemouth in 2007, David previously attended Milton Keynes College where he studied for a Foundation Diploma of art and design receiving a distinction for his efforts. As work has evolved over the three years, his working practice now revolves around an investigation into semiotics and colour. With a keen interest in collage and the use of the everyday found object, chance and automatism play significant roles within the working process. The photography, drawing, printing and painting are outcomes that he uses to construct a message consisting of a mix of primary and secondary research. The core of idea generation and decision-making comes from a critical evaluative writing process that occurs throughout practice.

1 Winning illustration

2 Sketches & Roughs

Gerald Durell

BRONZE

Lyn Moran

My Family & Other Animals

Stockport College of Further & Higher Education

Medium	Mono print, photography, texture, finish in Photoshop
Brief	Gerald Durell as a child in 1935. To encapsulate the feeling of nostalgia, and wonder of a young lads enjoyment in his new surroundings.
Course Leader	Gary Spicer
Course	BA (Hons) Design and Visual Art
Head of Department	Gary Spicer

Born in the UK, Lyn worked as a croupier for Playboy before moving to the USA where she worked as a personal trainer, window dresser, and back stage caterer before coming back to the UK. She really wanted to fulfil her dreams of being an illustrator and become a good role model for her little girl who has been her inspiration and reason for her life changing decisions.

237

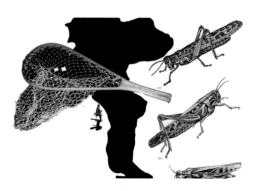

1 Winning illustration
2 Sketches & Roughs

Dave Bain
Snakes And Ladders (Illusion)

University College Falmouth

Medium	Acrylic on wood
Brief	To produce an alternative, exciting version of the traditional game, while retaining the original concept and theme.
Course Leader	Alan Male
Course	BA (Hons) Illustration

Lisa Marie Martin
An Allergy To Modern Life 1

University of Hertfordshire

Medium	Collage
Brief	From a series approaching the issue of excessive consumption and our need to constantly be buying to make us complete.
Course Leader	Paul Burgess
Course	BA Graphic Design & Illustration

Lisa Marie Martin
An Allergy To Modern Life 2

University of Hertfordshire

Medium	Collage
Brief	From a series approaching the issue of excessive consumption and our need to constantly be buying to make us complete.
Course Leader	Paul Burgess
Course	BA Graphic Design & Illustration

239

Jisun Lee
Hide And Seek

Kingston University

Medium	**Mixed**
Brief	**image for picture book.**
Course Leader	**Jake Abrams**
Course	**BA Illustration and Animation**

Jisun Lee
Monster

Kingston University

Medium	**Oil pastel, acrylic**
Brief	**Image for the picture book.**
Course Leaders	**Geoff Grandfield and Colin Myer**
Course	**BA Illustration and Animation**

Jisun Lee
Together

Kingston University

Medium	**Mixed**
Brief	**image for picture book.**
Course Leader	**Jake Abrams**
Course	**BA Illustration and Animation**

Jisun Lee
Socks

Kingston University

Medium	**Mixed**
Brief	**image for picture book.**
Course Leader	**Jake Abrams**
Course	**BA Illustration and Animation**

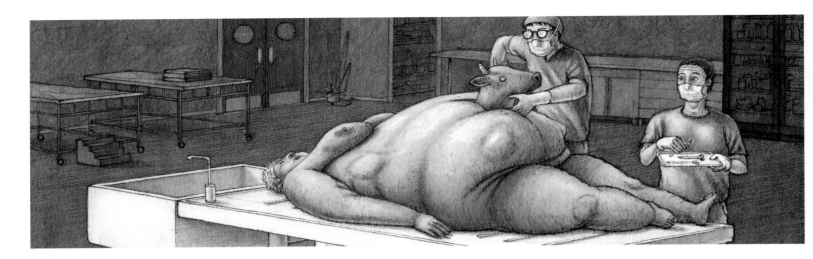

David Grinsted
The Post-Mortem Of An Old Lady

Norwich School of Art and Design

Medium	Watercolour, pen and coloured pencil
Brief	Produce a sequence of images for a book reinterpreting the classic children's poem 'The Old Woman Who Swallowed A Fly' for a more mature audience.
Course Leader	Robert Shadbolt + Robert Mason
Course	BA Graphic Design (illustration)

David Grinsted
The Siamese Satsuma

Norwich School of Art and Design

Medium	Oil paint with collage
Brief	Produce artwork for a fictitious book featuring the stories of misshapen fruit and vegetables.
Course Leader	Robert Shadbolt + Robert Mason
Course	BA Graphic Design (illustration)

David Grinsted
The Conjuring Fisherman's Seaside Spectacular

Norwich School of Art and Design

Medium	Acrylic, ink and coloured pencil
Brief	Produce an imaginative piece of illustration using the theme of 'the sea'.
Course Leader	Robert Shadbolt + Robert Mason
Course	BA Graphic Design (illustration)

BLACKPOOL NORTH PIER PROUDLY PRESENTS

THE CONJURING FISHERMAN'S SEASIDE
SPECTACULAR

Under the sole management of D. Grinsted

Showing every evening untill April - Doors open at seven o'clock precisely - Tickets are five Squid each

STARRING
The Famous
FIRE-BREATHING FLOUNDER!!

"Never before has there been an act of this nature."

THE KNOTTED EELS

The world renowned

MUSSEL MEN
OF MARGATE

THE GOLFIN' DOLPHIN

demonstrating his golfing talents each evening

The first appearance this season of
THE FISHMONGER'S
FLYING FERRET

"The most sensational achievement of the age!"

THE **OCTOPUS GIRL**

THE **BEARDED CRAB**

THE STICK OF ROCK THAT CANNOT LIE

and introducing the astounding wonder that is the great

GIANT
EGYPTIAN JELLY FISH

"ORIGINAL BEYOND ALL PRECEDENT"

◀ FEATURING ▶

STAND-UP COMEDY
WITH

PETRA
THE PENGUIN

BREATHTAKING MAGIC

BY THE
LEVITATING OYSTER

Astonishing
HYPNOSIS
with the
CANDY FLOSS KID

➤ **NO IMPROPER CHARACTERS ADMITTED - REFRESHMENTS OF THE CHOICEST QUALITY PROVIDED** ➤

Il Sung Na

Apart From A Staring Owl

Kingston University

Medium	Mixed media and Photoshop
Brief	Its a children's book about sleep. A curious owl shows you how the others sleep. Some snore, some stand up, some with open eyes...etc.
Course Leader	Geoff Grandfield
Course	BA Illustration and Animation

Il Sung Na

Some Make A Noise

Kingston University

Medium	Mixed media and Photoshop
Brief	Its a children's book about sleep. A curious owl shows you how the others sleep. Some snore, some stand up, some with open eyes...etc.
Course Leader	Geoff Grandfield
Course	BA Illustration and Animation

Il Sung Na

Some Sleep Upside Down

Kingston University

Medium	Mixed media and Photoshop
Brief	Its a children's book about sleep. A curious owl shows you how the others sleep. Some snore, some stand up, some with open eyes...etc.
Course Leader	Geoff Grandfield
Course	BA Illustration and Animation

Chloe Mutton

The Forum Centre

Dundee University

Medium	Mixed media / digital
Brief	Explore the 'disappearing world' of the indoor market shopping environment.
Course Leader	Mick Peter/ Donna Leishman
Course	BA Illustration

Sarah Knight
Wet Dream

University of Plymouth

Medium	Silk-screen print
Brief	Image from a self-authored narrative depicting the unusual relationship held between a man and an octopus.
Course Leader	Ashley Potter
Course	BA (hons) Design and Illustration

Sarah Knight
Bear Head

University of Plymouth

Medium	Silk-screen print
Course Leader	Ashley Potter
Course	BA (hons) Design and Illustration

Rachel Tudor Best
Bisque Doll And Cup

Hereford College of Art and Design

Medium	Ink, gouache, pencil, gold leaf
Brief	Selected from personal initiated work investigating the visual qualities of objects.
Course Leader	Emily Mitchell
Course	BA Hons Illustration

 Sarah Garson
The Grump

Cambridge School of Art

Medium	Watercolour
Brief	Woken by noises in the night, a boy searches the house encountering menacing shadows, huge footprints and a terrible mess... could it be The Grump?
Course Leader	Martin Salisbury
Course	MA Children's Book Illustration

Irene Fuga
Sloth

University of Westminster

Medium	Screenprint
Brief	Image inspired by the book 'Life of Pi' by Yann Martel.
Course Leader	Liz Grob
Course	BA (Hons) Illustration

 Irene Fuga
Bath

University of Westminster

Medium	Pen & ink drawing, collage
Brief	Drawing from the series 'Indelible Spaces', a personal project inspired by childhood memories.
Course Leader	Liz Grob
Course	BA (Hons) Illustration

249

Philip Hackett
Rachmaninov

Medium	Pen, paint and collage
Brief	Produce an image of Rachmaninov for an illustrated book on the great composers.
Course Leader	Emily Mitchell
Course	BA (hons) Illustration

Philip Hackett
Mozart

Medium	Pen, paint and collage
Brief	Produce an image of Mozart for an illustrated book on the great composers.
Course Leader	Emily Mitchell
Course	BA (hons) Illustration

Philip Hackett
Chopin

Medium	Pen, paint and collage
Brief	Produce an image of Chopin for an illustrated book on the great composers.
Course Leader	Emily Mitchell
Course	BA (hons) Illustration

Op. 53.

Rondeau: Op. 1 in G minor

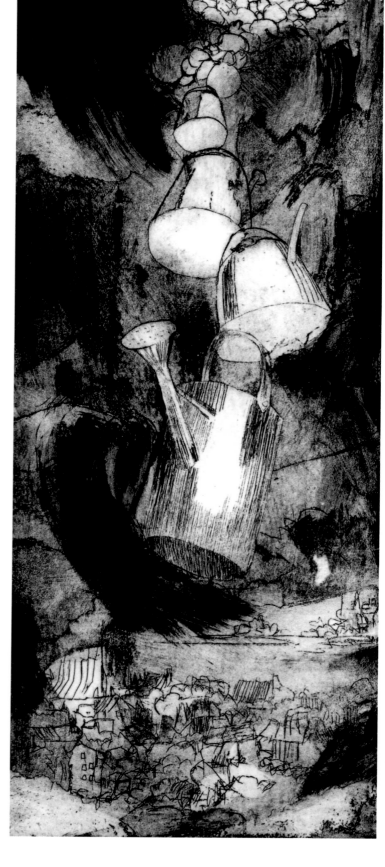

Noriko Oura

Face

Medium	**Illustrator/Photoshop**
Brief	**People have many faces. What kind of person are you today?**
Course Leader	**Paul Bowman**
Course	**BA Graphic Media Design, Illustration**

Fatime Szaszi

The Gale - Watercans Overflowed

Medium	**Print - aquatint and etching**
Brief	**College illustrated book project - *The Gale* by Bruno Schulz: "... watercans overflowed and swept through the night. Their black, shining, noisy concourse besieged the city."**
Course Leader	**Alan Male**
Course	**BA Illustration**

Amy Rowe

I Worried 01

Medium	**Photo montage**
Brief	**To illustrate the worries and paranoias that loved ones faced during World War II.**
Course Leader	**Ashley Potter**
Course	**BA Illustration**

 Amy Rowe
I Worried 02

University of Plymouth

Medium	**Photo montage**
Brief	**To illustrate the worries and paranoias that loved ones faced during World War II.**
Course Leader	**Ashley Potter**
Course	**BA Illustration**

253

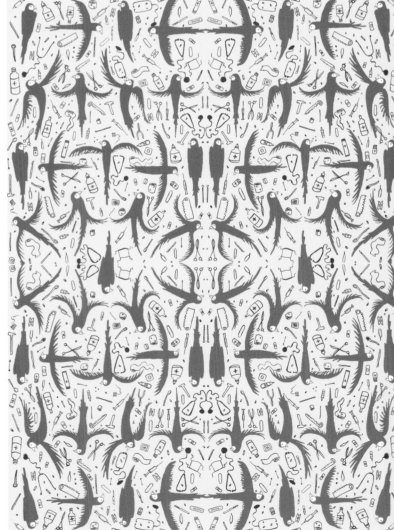

Caroline Ayello Wright
A Recipe For A Broken Mind

Kingston University

Medium	Chinese ink, paintbrush, digital
Brief	An illustration of a recipe, considering the role of text and image within the project.
Course Leader	Geoff Grandfield
Course	BA Hons Illustration with Animation

Caroline Ayello Wright
Sick As A Parrot

Kingston University

Medium	Chinese ink, paintbrush, digital
Brief	A pattern design in a series to illustrate animal metaphors.
Course Leader	Geoff Grandfield
Course	BA Hons Illustration with Animation

Gabriella Bianca
Cherryblossom

Central St Martins College of Art & Design

Medium	Photoshop
Brief	Illustration for "Get There Tonight" CD cover for electronic band with a full warm sound, stylish, forward thinking and globally minded.
Course Leader	Jayne Sanderson
Course	Computers for Fashion

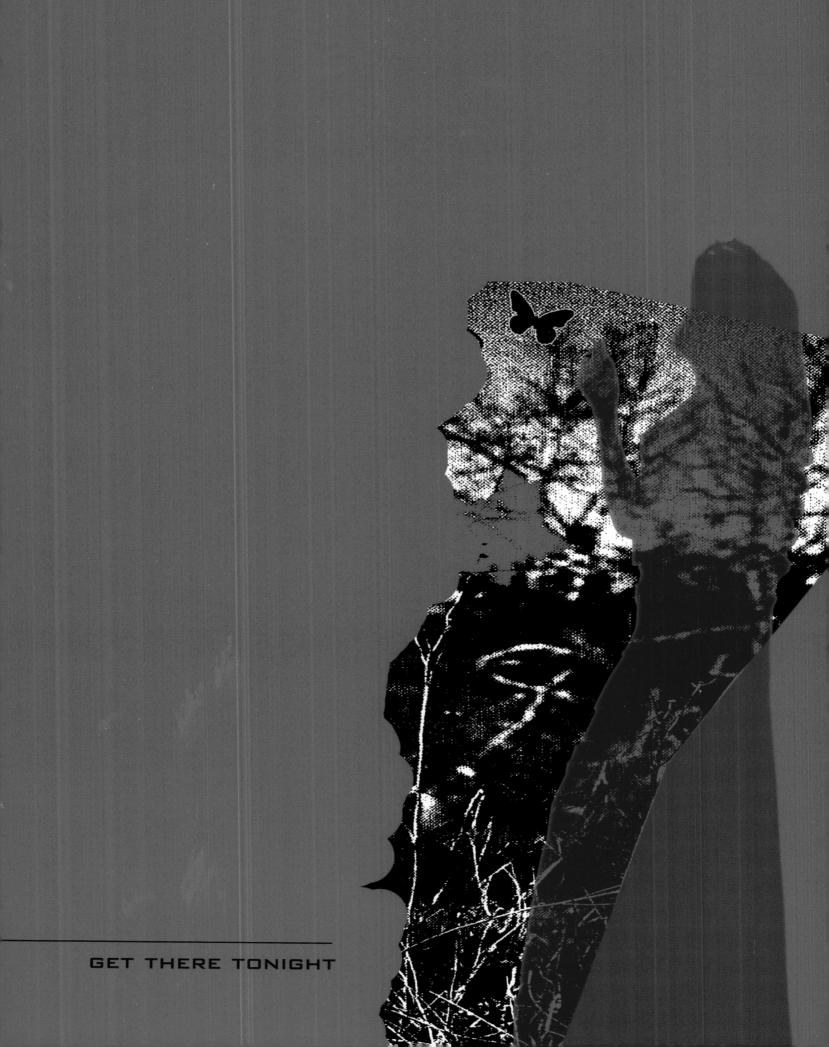

GET THERE TONIGHT

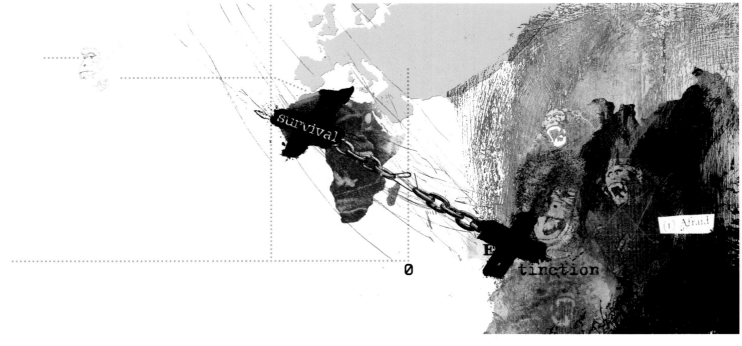

Chris Ede
Ask The Dust 1

University of Portsmouth

Medium	Mono print ink, photography, Photoshop
Brief	To create a book cover illustrating the gritty and tormented life of struggling writer Anturo Bandini, set in the 1930's. Deadline: 1 day.
Course Leader	Maureen O'Neill
Course	BA (Hons) Illustration

Chris Ede
Apes Plunge Towards Extinction

University of Portsmouth

Medium	Oil paint, cellulose thinner, pen, photocopies, Photoshop
Brief	Editorial highlighting how close we are to the extinction of our nearest ancestors. The chain is merely held together by a paper clip.
Course Leader	Maureen O'Neill
Course	BA (Hons) Illustration

Chris Ede
Ask The Dust 2

University of Portsmouth

Medium	Mono print ink, photography, Photoshop
Brief	Book cover illustrating the gritty and struggling life of writer Anturo Bandini, set in the 1930's. Deadline 1 day.
Course Leader	Maureen O'Neill
Course	BA (Hons) Illustration

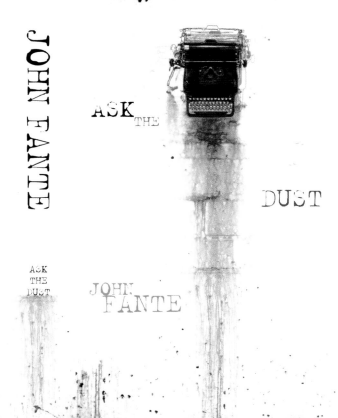

"Written of and from the gut and the heart... Fante was my god."
CHARLES BUKOWSKI

Arturo Bandini is a struggling writer lodging in a seedy LA hotel. While basking in the glory of having had a single short story published in a small magazine, he meets local waitress Camilla Lopez and they embark on a strange and strained love-hate relationship. Slowly, but inexorably, it descends into the realms of madness.

Ask the Dust is one of the truly great, yet unsung, American novels of the twentieth century. A tough and unsentimental story with a soft and tender heart, it remains as fresh and affecting as the day it was written.

"The late John Fante is one of the great unheralded voices in American fiction." **THE FACE**

"Bandini is a magnificent creation, and his rediscovery is not before time." **TIMES LITERARY SUPPLEMENT**

"A criminally neglected American writer." **TIME OUT**

"This stunning novel, as Bukowski's foreword outlines, was the reason he became a writer. Is there any better recommendation?" **UNCUT**

JOHN FANTE

ASK THE DUST

JOHN FANTE

ASK THE DUST

ISBN 1 84195 330 X
£6.99

9 781841 953304

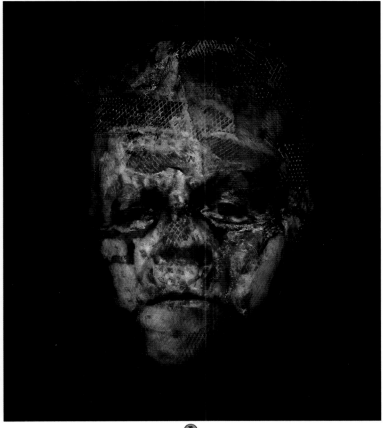

 PENGUIN CLASSICS

MARY SHELLEY

Frankenstein

Chris Ede
Frankenstein's Creation
University of Portsmouth

Medium	Papier mache, latex, chicken wire, ink, cloth, photography, Photoshop
Brief	Self directed project with a deadline of 2 weeks. Book cover illustration for Mary Shelly's 'Frankenstein'. Image showing the repulsiveness of the monster juxtaposed with it's human qualities.
Course Leader	Maureen O'Neill
Course	BA (Hons) Illustration

    Robert Conway
Pub

Stafford College

Medium	Charcoal and acrylic
Brief	Produced from sketches drawn on location in the local pub.
Course Leader	Iain Lowe
Course	HND Illustration

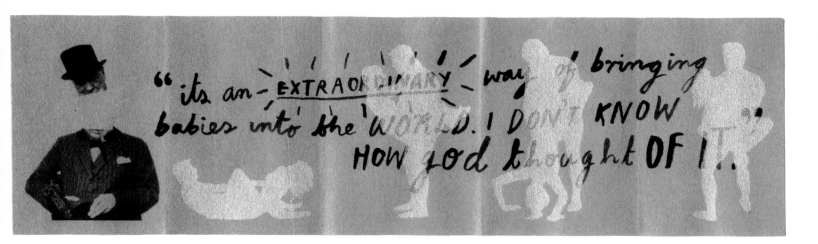

259

 Robert Conway
Promenade Stroll

Stafford College

Medium	Mixed media
Brief	One in a series of images illustrating Blackpool's low season. This picture focuses on the daily routine of local residents.
Course Leader	Iain Lowe
Course	HND Illustration

Jessica Wilson
Business Card

Buckinghamshire Chilterns University College

Medium	Screen print
Brief	Produce a Business Card to promote Final Major Project. A magazine called 'Sorry', about eccentric British culture.
Course Leader	Dan Williams/Bruce Ingman
Course	Graphic Design and Advertising

 Alice Wood
The Den In The Woods

Cambridge School of Art

Medium	Pen and watercolour
Brief	Picture book about a little girl, Ruby Green, who finds a nest of baby woodpeckers inside a hollow tree in the woods, near her home.
Course Leader	Martin Salisbury
Course	MA Children's Book Illustration

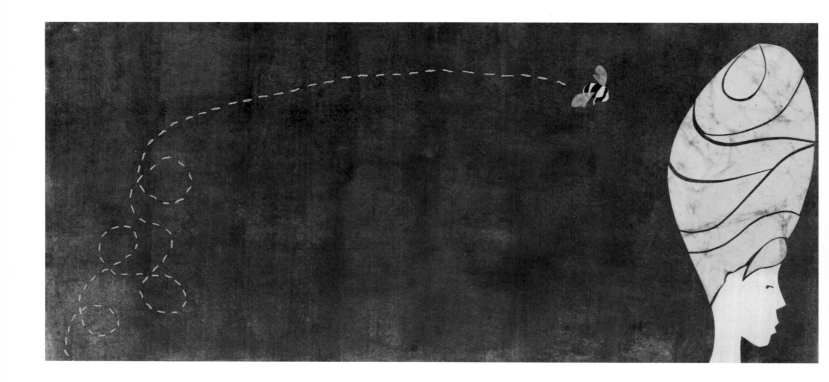

Alexandra Gardner
Bee Seeing You

Loughborough University, School of Art
And Design

Medium	Collage and paint
Brief	A New Scientist article discussing if a bee could find its way home after flying onto a train, then flying off further down the line.
Course Leader	Andrew Selby
Course	BA (Hons) Illustration (with Animation)

Louisa Jones
Brazilian Series

Camberwell College of Art

Medium	Black pen and collage
Brief	'Brazilian Series' is a sequence of drawings that communicate my impressions and experiences during my recent travels in Brazil. It illustrates my journey and aims to convey a sense of the beauty and diversity I found there.
Course Leader	Mark Wigan
Course	BA (Hons) Illustration

Ceri Watling

Noise

University of Central Lancashire

Medium	Collage, spraypaint, acrylic, printmaking
Brief	Entry for Mercury Music Prize Art Award. Create an image inspired by music, to be used as a CD cover illustration.
Course Leader	Steve Wilkin
Course	BA (Hons) Illustration

Ceri Watling

What Lies Beneath?

University of Central Lancashire

Medium	Digital collage, spraypaint, printmaking
Brief	Illustration based on an article in Fortean Times about an Italian lake monster which also featured sealions and UFOs.
Course Leader	Steve Wilkin
Course	BA (Hons) Illustration

Cheryl Taylor

The Cost Of Train Travel

Stockport College of Further & Higher Education

Medium	Illustrator, Photoshop, found imagery
Brief	This illustration was for an editorial about how train travel was becoming so dear it would only be available to the rich and elite.
Course Leader	Ian Murray
Course	BA (Hons) dsesign and Visual Arts - Illustration

Cheryl Taylor

Anger

Stockport College of Further & Higher Education

Medium	Illustrator, Photoshop, spray paint, found imagery
Brief	To show the main consequence of anger, and how it effects the people around you, and what devastating effect it has.
Course Leader	Ian Murray
Course	BA (Hons) dsesign and Visual Arts - Illustration

 Jaimi Lee Cameron Stewart
Escape! Circle City Street Scene

Cumbria Institute of the Arts

Medium	Embroidered textile/multimedia
Brief	The following imagery are photographs of a movable set created from a story I wrote and illustrated.
Course Leader	Angie Wyman
Course	BA (Hons) Contemporary Applied Arts

Jaimi Lee Cameron Stewart
Escape! Circle City Street Scene

Cumbria Institute of the Arts

Medium	**Embroidered textile/multimedia**
Brief	**The following imagery are photographs of a moveable set created from a story I wrote and illustrated.**
Course Leader	**Angie Wyman**
Course	**BA (Hons) Contemporary Applied Arts**

Alex Strang
Frau Lefmann July 1965

London College of Communication

Medium	**Pencil, pencil crayon**
Brief	**Based on found photographs using found material (pack of crayons and graph paper, previously a note pad) making the most of limited resources.**
Course Leader	**Paul Bowman**
Course	**BA Graphic Media Design, Illustration**

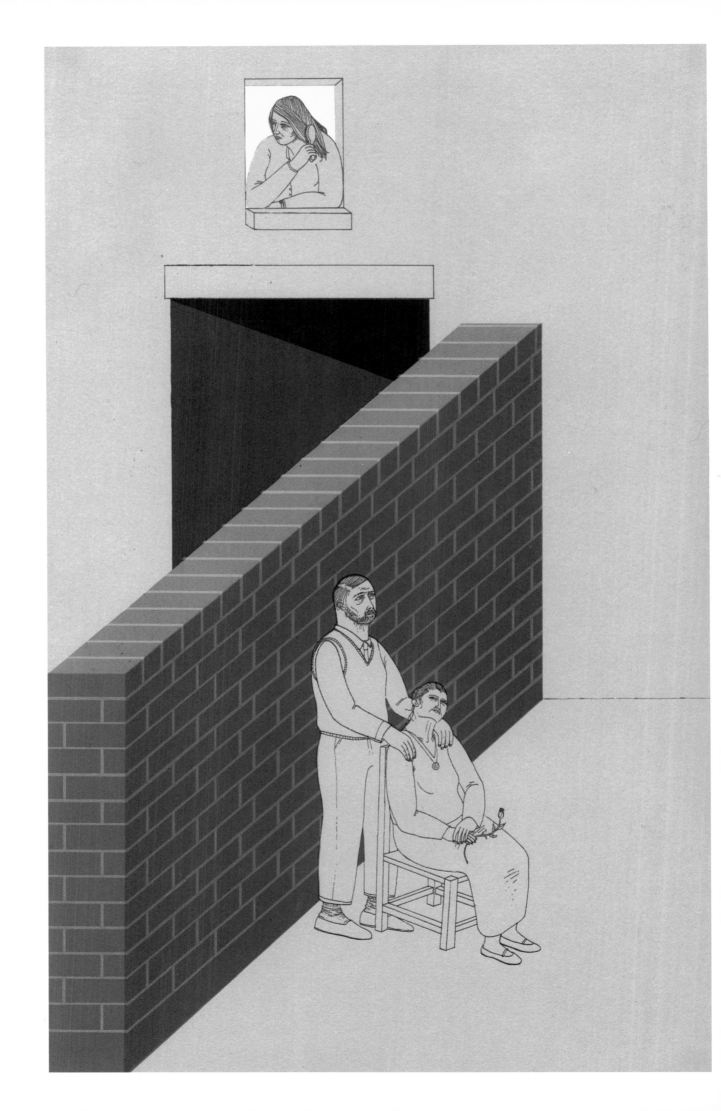

Michael Kirkham
War

Medium	Screenprint
Brief	To tell the pictorial equivalent of a short story.
Course Leader	Jonathan Gibbs
Course	illustration

Debbie Powell
Untitled

Medium	Silkscreen
Brief	Accompanying illustration for a short story based on the ideology of Ivana Helsinki clothing.
Course Leader	Amanda Evans
Course	BA Illustration

Debbie Powell
Untitled

Medium	Silkscreen
Brief	Accompanying illustration for a short story based on the ideology of Ivana Helsinki clothing.
Course Leader	Amanda Evans
Course	BA Illustration

 Chris Burge
Vegetable Pig

University College Falmouth

Medium	**Gouache/acrylic/digital**
Brief	**Illustration to accompany the quote 'If God intended us to be vegetarian, why did he make animals out of meat?'**
Course Leader	**Alan Male**
Course	**BA (Hons) Illustration**

 Chris Burge
Alice In Wonderland

University College Falmouth

Medium	**Gouache/collage/digital**
Brief	**Illustration for Lewis Carroll's children's book 'Alice's Adventures in Wonderland', to appeal to both adults and children.**
Course Leader	**Alan Male**
Course	**BA (Hons) Illustration**

269

Yee Ting Kuit
Quotes

University College Falmouth

Medium	Digital
Brief	To create an illustration based on a proverb: 'A book is like a garden carried in the pocket', that represented my style of work.
Course Leader	Alan Male
Course	BA (Hons) Illustration

Rachel Horton
'Yorkshire Folk'

Loughborough University, School of Art And Design

Medium	Mixed media- polymer clay, various fabrics and photography.
Brief	Image from a narrative series based on stereotypical 'Yorkshire Folk'. This image is the Ye olde pub scene.
Course Leader	Paul Wells
Course	MA Art & Design (studio practice)

Jade Perry
untitled

Central St Martins College of Art & Design

Medium	Pencil
Brief	Exploring mood and character through enlargement and overlaying of elements, to evoke an atmosphere which speaks of solitude and contemplation.
Course Leader	Andrew Foster
Course	MA Communication Design

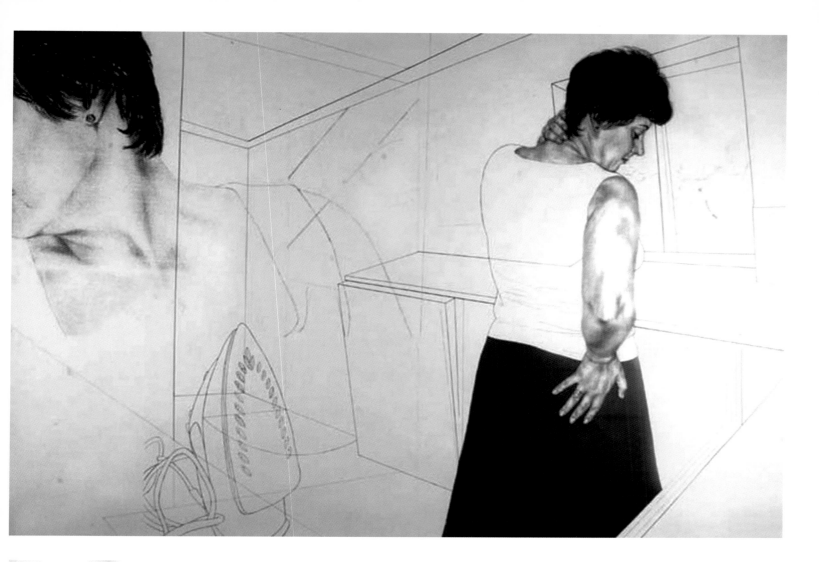

 Jade Perry
Young Buck

Central St Martins College of Art & Design

Medium	Pencil
Brief	Looking at human and animal behaviour, a set of anthropomorphic images were created to reflect certain characteristics of family members.
Course Leader	Andrew Foster
Course	MA Communication Design

 Andrea Speakman
Venus Flytrap

Blackpool and the Fylde

Medium	Adobe Illustrator
Course Leader	Robert Cook
Course	BA Scientific and Natural History Illustration

 Paul Smith
There Was An Old Man...

University of Sunderland

Medium	Collage/pen and ink
Brief	Self-set final year project - an illustrated book of a number of the limericks of Edward Lear and others.
Course Leader	Alison Barratt
Course	BA & MA Illustration & Design

 Jody Boehnert
Blue Girl In Heels

London College of Communication

Medium	Ink
Brief	Expose awkward reality of high heels.
Course Leader	Russell Bestley
Course	MA Graphics

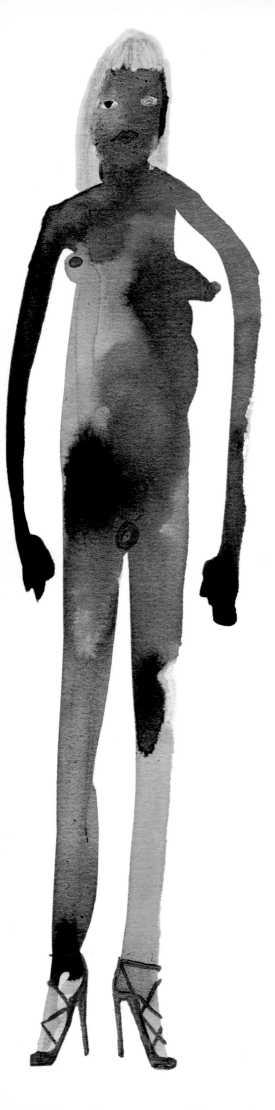

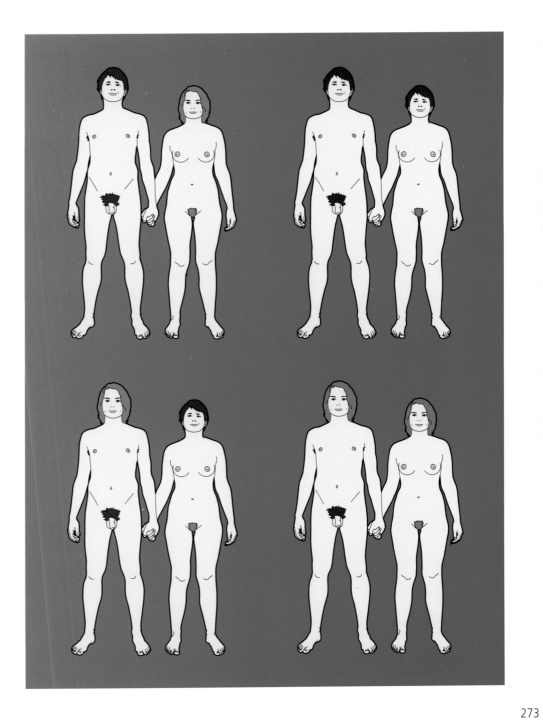

Solveig Rolfsdottir
Couples

Camberwell College of Arts

Medium	Digital vector drawing
Brief	Made for an exhibition. Theme: Hybridity, Identity & the Self. The individualis identity follows the face while the gender is attached to the body.
Course Leader	Janet Woolley
Course	MA Illustration

Rebecca Bromley
A Good Poem

Medium	Collage/drawn
Brief	Illustration for a jointly compiled book by students in Kingston university class of 2006- illustrating 'a good poem' by Charles Bukowski. Line: 'death melts like hot butter'.
Course Leader	Geoff Grandfield
Course	BA (Hons) Illustration with Animation

Jacqueline Wagner
Every Child Knew There Were Certain Questions You Wouldn't Ask In School

Medium	Digital collage
Brief	Series of Editorial illustrations about a childhood in Socialism.
Course Leader	Paul Bowman
Course	BA (Hons) Graphic and Media Design, Illustration

Jenny Simms
The Erl King

Medium	Digital collage
Brief	A full page illustration for 'The Erl King', a short story from 'The Bloody Chamber' by Angela Carter.
Course Leader	Derek Rodgers
Course	BA (Hons) Illustration

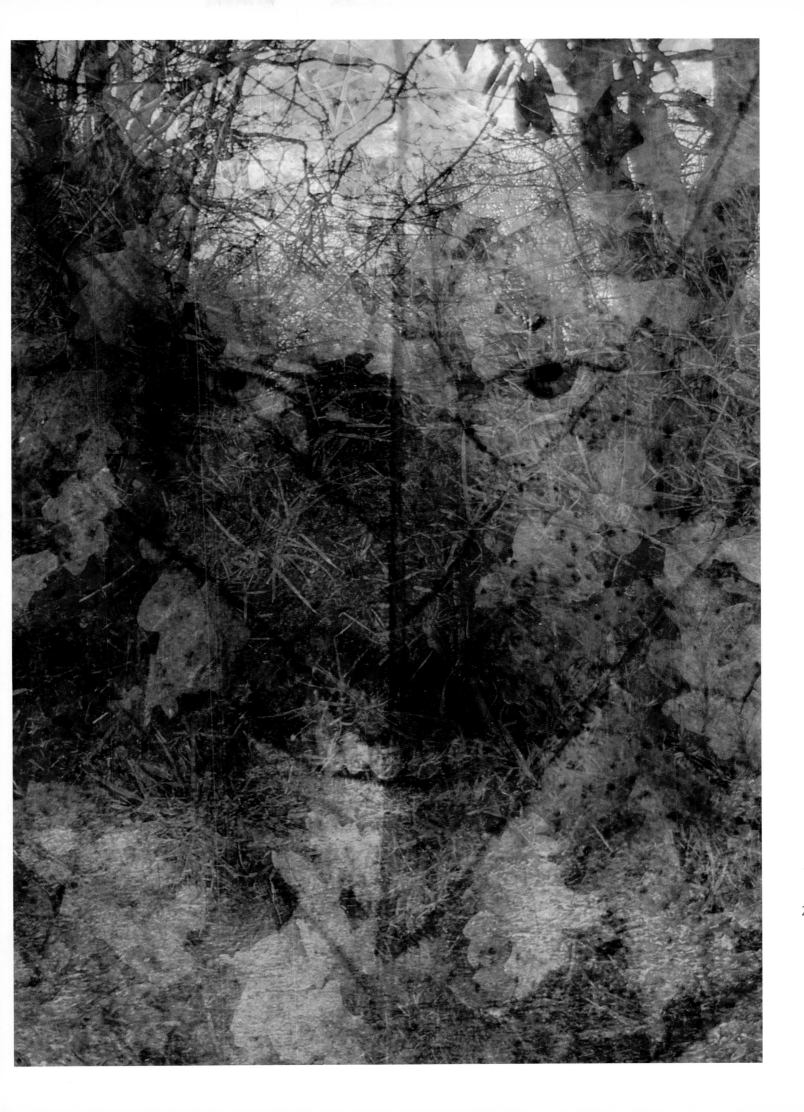

Michelle Bower
Penguin Redesigns

Loughborough University, School of Art
And Design

Medium	Ink, dip-pen and digital
Brief	Redesign iconic Penguin book covers to make the penguin the focus of the illustration.
Course Leader	Andrew Selby
Course	Visual Communication - Illustration

Valérie Pézeron
D.N.A - The National Dyslexics Association

Kingston University

Medium	Mixed media, collage and Photoshop.
Brief	To illustrate an article titled D.N.A written by journalist Daniela about her dyslexia and about how the education system fails dyslexic people.
Course Leader	Colin Meir
Course	BA Illustration & Animation

Valérie Pézeron
Written By Men, Blame It On God

Kingston University

Medium	Felt tip pen, collage and Photoshop
Brief	Image created for a graphic novel about the description and treatment of women in the Bible and Catholic religion.
Course Leader	Colin Meir
Course	BA Illustration & Animation

This is JERMALLE
he is a **rastafarian**
he smokes weed alot of the
time and hasn't washed his hair
for **20 years**

Angus Campbell
Figures In Landscape
Biad, Uce, Birmingham

Medium	Acrylic/gouache on canvas
Brief	To create a series of pictures featuring characters in an environment that create a sense of menace.
Course Leader	George Hart
Course	BA Visual Communication

Nicholas Reyniers
Stereotypes
Camberwell College of Arts

Medium	Print
Brief	These images are from a series of 50 character designs entitled 'Stereotypes' created for animation.
Course Leader	Mark Wigan
Course	BA (Hons.) Illustration

Emma Robinson
The Pursuit of Love
Hereford College of Art and Design

Medium	Collage
Brief	Book cover design for the fantastic snapshot of a bygone age.
Course Leader	Emily Mitchell
Course	BA (Hons) Illustration

The Pursuit of Love

Nancy Mitford

 Poul Rennolf

Panthera Tigris Altaica

York College

Medium	**Graphite pencil**
Brief	**To produce a finely detailed drawing for a personal portfolio in order to gain entry into higher education.**
Course Leader	**Jan Kaliciak**
Course	**Graphic Design**

 Tom Cornfoot

Burlesque Poster

University of Hertfordshire

Medium	**Collage**
Brief	**To use ephemera and found image to create a new illustration for use in the promotion of a burlesque or circus show.**
Course Leader	**Paul Burgess**
Course	**BA Graphic Design & Illustration**

281

Index of illustrators

A = Agent, T = Telephone, F = Fax, M = Mobile, E = Email, W = Website. To call from outside the UK add the prefix '44' and omit the first '0' from the number provided.

Nathan Daniels   164-165
Centrespace
6 Leonard Lane
Bristol
BS1 1EA
M 07833 122 476
E nathan@nathandaniels.com
W www.nathandaniels.com

Andrew Davidson   52-53
Moors Cottage
Swells Hill
Brimscombe
Stroud
Gloustershire
GL5 2SP
T 01453 884 650
E andrew@swellshill.demon.co.uk
A Stephanie Alexander
The Artworks
2nd Floor
40 Frith Street
London
W1D 5LN
T 020 7734 3333
E steph@theartworksinc.com

Andy Davies   133
14 Wyebank Place
Tutshill
Chepstow
Monmouthshire
NP16 7EU
T 01291 625 968
M 07961 068 227
E andy@ardillustration.com
W www.ardillustration.com

Tom Denbigh   139
Pondsmeade Cottage
Water End Lane
Redbourn
Herts
AL3 7JZ
T 01582 792 608
M 07974 748 787
E tomdenbigh@hotmail.com
W www.tomdenbigh.com

Sarah Dickie   152
16a Claremont Road
Surbiton
Surrey
KT6 4QU
M 07855 476 115
E sarah@sarahdickie.com
W www.sarahdickie.com

Darren Diss   190
E darrendiss@yahoo.co.uk
W www.darrendissillustrator.co.uk
A The Art Market
51 Oxford Drive
London
SE1 2FB
W www.artmarketillustration.com

Ian Dodds   48-49
5 Brownsea Close
Rubery
Rednal
Birmingham
B45 0HH
M 07905 243 739
E contact@iandodds.co.uk
W www.iandodds.co.uk

Chris Ede   256-257
9 Martlet Close
Chichester
West Sussex
PO19 8DF
M 07813 262 220
E edeos@hotmail.com
W www.chrisede.com

Max Ellis   154
60 Clonmel Road
Teddington
Middlesex
TW11 0SR
T 020 8977 8924
M 07976 242 378
E max@junkyard.co.uk
W www.junkyard.co.uk
A Central Illustration Agency
36 Wellington Street
London
WC2E 7BD
T 020 7240 8925
W www.centralillustration.com

Mike Ellis   129
29 Hills Farm Lane
Horsham
West Sussex
RH12 1TZ
M 07799 099 1862
E michael.ellis@hotmail.com

Sara Fanelli   42-43
1st Floor
45 Belsize Avenue
London
NW3 4BN
T 020 7794 4533
F 020 7794 4533
E sara@sarafanelli.com
W www.sarafanelli.com

Anna - Louise Felstead MA (RCA)   191
M 07887 714 637
E info@alfelstead.com
W www.alfelstead.com

Fine-n-Dandy   231
Riverside 10
Sheaf Bank Works
Prospect Road
Sheffield
S2 3EN
T 0 11 42 58 22 66
E pat@studio-dust.com
W www.studio-dust.com
A Central Illustration Agency
36 Wellington Street
London
WC2E 7BD
T 020 7240 8925
W www.centralillustration.com

Jessie Ford   193
Studio 6
Great Western Studios
Great Western Road
London
W9 3NY
M 07980 735 153
E missjessief@yahoo.co.uk
W www.jessieford.co.uk
A Central Illustration Agency
36 Wellington Street
London
WC2E 7BD
T 020 7240 8925
W www.centralillustration.com

James Fryer   170-171
160 Lower Farnham Road
Aldershot
Hampshire
GU12 4EL
T 01252 671 377
M 07812 672 819
F 01252 671 377
E james_fryer72@ntlworld.com
W www.jamesfryer.co.uk

Irene Fuga   248-249
2nd Floor Flat
90 Fordwych Road
London
NW2 3TJ
M 07748 141 199
E irene.fuga@gmail.com

Chris Garbutt   155
A Arena
31 Eleanor Road
London
E15 4AB
T 0845 050 7600
E info@arenaworks.com
W www.arenaworks.com

Alexandra Gardner   260
31 Park Hill
Harpenden
Hertfordshire
AL5 3AT
T 01582 764 702
M 07793 972 304
E alex_gardner@hotmail.com

Sarah Garson   248
110 Banbury Road
Oxford
OX2 6JU
T 01865 310 928
M 07775 627 828
E sarah.garson@gmail.com
W www.sarahgarson.com

Tom Gaul   132
43 Hawkwood Crescent
Chingford
London
E4 7PH
T 020 8524 7023
M 07960 010 073
E gauly82@talk21.com
W www.tomgaul.com

Sarah Gibb   203
A The Artworks
2nd Floor
40 Frith Street
London
W1D 5LN
T 020 7734 3333
E steph@theartworksinc.com
W www.theartworksinc.com

Christopher Gibbs   16-17, 44
54 Brands Hill Avenue
High Wycombe
Buck
HP13 5PU
E mc_c_lone@hotmail.com
W www.Arenaworks.com
A Arena
31 Eleanor Road
London
E15 4AB
T 0845 050 7600
E info@arenaworks.com
W www.arenaworks.com

Jonathan Gibbs   37, 134
Farmhouse
Keith Marischal
Humbie
East Lothian
EH36 5PA
T 01875 833 346
F 0131 2216 100
E j.gibbs@eca.ac.uk
A Central Illustration Agency
36 Wellington Street
London
WC2E 7BD
T 020 7240 8925
W www.centralillustration.com

Purdi Gibson   195
66 Seville Street
Royton
Lancashire
OL2 6AN
T 0161 287 9989
M 07921 672 942
E petunia@purdi.net
W www.purdi.net

Fossil Glanville   172-173
107 Hungerford Road
Holloway
London
N7 9LD
T 020 7607 8424
M 07855 066 482
E fossilglanville@yahoo.co.uk
W www.fossilglanville.com

Adam Graff   65
7 Rushbrook Crescent
London
E17 5BZ
T 020 8531 1238
M 07747 196 811
E a_graff@btinternet.com
W www.adamgraff.co.uk
A Eye Candy
Pepperpot Corner
Manor Yard, Blithbury Road
Hamshall Ridmore
Staffs
WS15 3RS
W www.eyecandy.co.uk

Geoff Grandfield   178-179
30 Allen Road
London
N16 8SA
T 020 7241 1523
M 07831 534 192
E geoff@geoffgrandfield.co.uk
W www.geoffgrandfield.co.uk

Willi Gray   133
9 York Street
Norwich
Norfolk
NR2 2AN
T 01603 499 928
M 07960 896 037
E gris.gris@ntlworld.com

Brian Grimwood   206
10 Church Hill
Patcham
Brighton
BN1 8YE
M 07702 955 388
E brian@briangrimwood.com
W www.briangrimwood.com
A Central Illustration Agency
36 Wellington Street
London
WC2E 7BD
T 020 7240 8925
E info@centralillustration.com
W www.centralillustration.com

David Grinsted   242-243
355 Rush Green Road
Romford
Essex
RM7 0NJ
M 07961 950 622
E davidgrinsted@yahoo.co.uk
W www.davidgrinsted.moonfruit.com

Peter Grundy   192
Studio 69
1 Town Meadow
Brentford
Middlesex
TW8 0BQ
T 020 8384 1076
M 07769 703 844
E peter@grundini.com
W www.grundini.com

Philip Hackett   250-251
5 Collingwood Court
Whittern Way
Hereford
HR1 1PH
M 07757 338 815
E hackettillustration@hotmail.co.uk
W www.eyecandy.co.uk
A Eye Candy
Pepperpot Corner
Manor Yard, Blithbury Road
Hamshall Ridmore
Staffs
WS15 3RS
T 020 8291 0729
W www.eyecandy.co.uk

Stephen Hall   222
Studio 7
3rd Floor
Proton House
4 Coburg Road
London
N22 6UJ
T 020 8829 8922
M 07976 125 111
E sh@digitillo.co.uk
W www.digitillo.co.uk

Christopher Halsall   221
91 Spelding Drive
Standish
Lower Ground
Wigan
Lancs
WN6 8LW
T 01942 321 389
M 07724 623 632
E chrishalsall@hotmail.com
W www.topherillustration.com

Jo Halstead   225
11 Parker Street
Oxford
Oxfordshire
OX4 1TD
T 01865 724 907
M 07929 232 907
E jojojoey_82@hotmail.com
W www.johalstead.com

Sarah Hanson   60,61
M 07739 987 306
E illustration@sarahhanson.co.uk
W www.sarahhanson.co.uk
A Debut Art
30 Tottenham Street
London
W1T 4RJ
T 020 7636 1064
W www.debutart.com

Swava Harasymowicz   194
168a Stroud Green Road
London
N4 3RS
T 020 7281 9682
M 07946 054 343
E swava@swavaharasymowicz.com
W www.swavaharasymowicz.com

Nick Hardcastle   163
April Cottage
The Rosery
Mulbarton
Norwich
Norfolk
NR14 8AL
T 01508 570 153
M 07973 144 696
F 01508 570 153
E nickhardcastle@supanet.com
W www.nickhardcastle.co.uk
A The Bright Agency
20 Bradmore Park Road
London
W6 0DS
T 020 8741 3334
E vicki@thebrightagency.com

Index of illustrators

A = Agent, T = Telephone, F = Fax, M = Mobile, E = Email, W = Website. To call from outside the UK add the prefix 44' and omit the first '0' from the number provided.

Frank Love   100
the dairy studios
154 Heavitree Road
Exeter
EX1 2LZ
T 01392 432 911
M 07930 492 471
E thedairystudios@btinternet.com
W www.thedairystudios.co.uk
A Eastwing
99 Chase Side
Enfield
EN2 6NL
T 020 8367 6760
W www.eastwing.co.uk

Nick Lowndes   88
40 Eaton Road
Sale
Cheshire
M33 7TZ
M 07773 933 348
E nick@nicklowndes.co.uk
A Eastwing
99 Chase Side
Enfield
EN2 6NL
T 020 8367 6760
W www.eastwing.co.uk

Peter Mac   228-229
The Annexe Studio
Belmont Street
Brighton
East Sussex
BN1 4HN
T 01273 706 914
E peter@brighton.co.uk
W www.peter-greenwood.com

Andrew MacGregor   207
Studio 1c
3 Torrens St
London
EC1V 1NQ
T 020 7837 4070
M 07880 556 646
E ask@andymacgregor.com
W www.andymacgregor.com
A Debut Art
30 Tottenham Street
London
W1T 4RJ
T 020 7636 1064
W www.debutart.com

Lucy MacLeod   219
A Private View (PVUK)
17a Swan Hill
Shrewsbury
Shropshire
SY1 1NL
T 01743 350 355
E create@pvuk.com
W www.pvuk.com

Tim Marrs   224
43 Vicarage Road
Hastings
TN34 3LZ
T 020 8653 8044
M 07714 062 447
E tim@timmarrs.co.uk
W www.timmarrs.co.uk
A Central Illustration Agency
36 Wellington Street
London
WC2E 7BD
T 020 7240 8925
W www.centralillustration.com

Lisa Marie Martin   239
36 Icknield Way
Baldock
Herts
SG7 5AL
T 01462 894 223
M 07719 935 841
E lisa.mariemartin@virgin.net
W www.penpaperscissors.co.uk

Sue Mason   217
14 Sydner Road
London
N16 7UG
M 07970 522 375
E info@suemason.net
W www.suemason.net
A Caroline Sheldon Literary Agency
70 - 75 Cowcross Street
London
EC1M 6EJ

Steve May   199
61a Old Bethnal Green Road
London
E2 6QA
M 07790 033 786
E info@arenaworks.com
W www.arenaworks.com
A Arena
31 Eleanor Road
London
E15 4AB
T 0845 050 7600
E info@arenaworks.com
W www.arenaworks.com

David McConochie   40
96 Aylesford Mews
Sunderland
Tyne And Wear
SR2 9HZ
T 01915 100 702
M 07970 613 130
E davidmcconochie@hotmail.com
W www.davidmcconochie.co.uk
A The Art Market
51 Oxford Drive
London
SE1 2FB
W www.artmkt.co.uk

Shane McG   177
W www.shanemcgworld.com
A Three in a Box (Canada)
862 Richmond Street West
Suite 201
Toronto
Canada
T 020 8853 1236
W www.threeinabox.com

Hannah McVicar   220
Rose Cottage
Shellards Lane
Alveston
Bristol
BS35 3SY
T 01454 413 737
M 07740 841 186
E illustration@hannahmcvicar.co.uk
W www.hannahmcvicar.co.uk

Belle Mellor   110-111
Flat 3
12 Lansdowne Street
Hove
East Sussex
BN3 1FQ
T 01273 220 839
M 07973 463 942
F 01273 220 839
E belle.mellor@virgin.net
W www.bellemellor.com
A Three In A Box
862 Richmond Street West
Suite 201
Toronto
Canada
W www.threeinabox.com

Jasmine Mercer   107
Flat 4
59 Hova Villas
Hove
East Sussex
BN3 3DJ
T 01273 328 266
M 07947 244 423
E treefrog_illustration@hotmail.com
W www.treefrogillustration.co.uk

Adria Meserve   208
14 Dunsmure Road
Stamford Hill
London
N16 5PW
T 020 7502 6368
M 07944 501 352
E adria.meserve@blueyonder.co.uk

Kate Miller   56
41 Raeburn Place
Edinburgh
EH4 1HX
T 0131 332 1883
M 07958 998 078
F 0131 332 1883
E kate@kate-miller.com
W www.kate-miller.com
A Central Illustration Agency
36 Wellington Street
London
WC2E 7BD
T 020 7240 8925
W www.centralillustration.com

Lyn Moran   237
31 Avanley Crescent
Bridgehall
Syockport
Cheshire
SK3 8NH
T 0161 612 1183
M 07783 109 740
E lynmoran622@yahoo.co.uk

Ayako Morisawa   208
1293 Kamiijiri
Enzan
Kousyu-shi
Yamanashi
404-0046
Japan
T +81 553 332 118
F +81 553 332 118
E ayaaya327@hotmail.com
W www.ayako-m.com
A Artistop
W www.artistop.co.uk/index.asp

Matt Murphy   76
6 Lenthay Road
Sherbourne
Dorset
DT9 6AA
T 01935 817 751
M 07876 593 841
E matt@blackcoffeeproject.com
W www.blackcoffeeproject.com

Chloe Mutton   245
77 Frietuna Road
Frinton-On-Sea
Essex
CO13 0QP
T 01255 850 588
M 07739 314 732
E chloe.mutton@btinternet.com
W www.chloe-mutton-illustration.com

Il Sung Na   244-245
Flat A
101 Messina Avenue
London
NW6 4LG
M 07702 497 804
E ilsungna@hotmail.com
W www.ilsungna.com

Jenny Noscoe   77
19A Beaucroft Lane
Colehill
Wimborne
Dorset
BH21 2PF
T 01202 880 631
M 07834 233 343
E jen_neefer@yahoo.com
W www.jennynoscoe.co.uk

Sara Nunan   213
201 Westbourne Studios
242 Acklam Road
London
W10 5JJ
M 07973 852 895
E sara@saranunan.co.uk

Henry Obasi   82
PPaint
Unit 27 Links Yard
29a Spelman Street
London
E1 5LX
T 020 7247 9863
M 07909 904 400
E henry@ppaint.net
W www.ppaint.net

Orly Orbach   216
11 South End Road
London
NW3 2PT
T 020 7435 4625
M 07971 793 684
E info@orlyorbach.com
W www.orlyorbach.com

Dettmer Otto   74
Studio 2
Space Studios
142 - 170 Vauxhall Street
London
SE11 5RH
M 07979 952 982
E otto@ottoillustration.com
W www.ottoillustration.com

Noriko Oura   252
135 Chartridge House
Westmoreland Road
London
SE17 2DA
M 07806 462 814
E info@norikooura.com
W www.norikooura.com

Dandi Palmer   215
9 Albert Road
Folkestone
Kent
CT19 5RF
T 01303 242 246
F 01303 242 246
E dandipalmer@tiscali.co.uk
W www.dandi.me.uk/folio

Garry Parsons   80-81
Studio 002
2 Limesford Road
London
SE15 3BX
T 020 7732 4481
M 07931 923 934
F 020 7732 4481
E bachimitsu@btconnect.com
W www.garryparsons.co.uk
A Meiklejohn Illustration
5 Risborough Street
London
SE1 0HF

Jackie Parsons   211
Cut It Out Ltd
Studio & Gallery
9 Marine Court
St Leonards on Sea
East Sussex
TN38 0DX
T 01424 441 972
M 07957 121 818
F 01424 441 972
E parsons@dircon.co.uk
W www.jackieparsons.com
A Central Illustration Agency
36 Wellington Street
London
WC2E 7BD
T 020 7240 8925
W www.centralillustration.com

Matt Pattinson   212
Flat 1 Fr
47 Spottiswood St
Marchmont
Edinburgh
EH9 IDQ
M 07816 413 521
E mattpatt.520@virgin.net

Simon Pemberton   30, 184-185
A Heart Agency
Top Floor
100 De Beauvoir Road
London
N1 4EN
T 020 7254 5558
E info@heartagency.com
W www.heartagency.com

Jade Perry   271
62 Stockton Close
Hadleigh
Suffolk
IP7 5SH
T 01473 824 439
M 07708 481 124
E jadeperry5@hotmail.com
W www.jadeperry.co.uk

Valérie Pézeron   277
1B Wyatt Park Road
Streatham Hill
London
SW2 3TN
M 07909 561 055
E vay_4@yahoo.com
W www.valochedesigns.com

Sally Pinhey   64
664 Dorchester Road
Upwey
Dorset
DT3 5LE
T 01305 813 307
M 07719 923 434
F 01305 813 307
E sallypinhey@tiscali.co.uk
W www.sallypinhey.com

Ian Pollock   75
171 Bond Street
Macclesfield
Cheshire
SK11 6RE
T 01625 426 205
M 07770 927 940
F 01625 426 205
E ianpllck@aol.com
W www.ianpollock.co.uk
A The Inkshed
99 Chase Side
Enfield
London
EN2 6NL

Ashley Potter   12
the dairy studios
154 Heavitree Road
Exeter
EX1 2LZ
T 01392 432 911
M 07930 492 471
E thedairystudios@btinternet.com
W www.thedairystudios.co.uk

Alice Potterton   199
35 Briar Close
Evesham
Worcestershire
WR11 4JJ
T 0138 648 363
M 07990 687 670
E alice@alicepalace.co.uk
W www.alicepalace.co.uk

A = Agent, T = Telephone, F = Fax, M = Mobile, E = Email, W = Website. To call from outside the UK add the prefix 44' and omit the first '0' from the number provided.

the AOI would like to **Thank**

...all members of the jury for applying their expertise to the difficult task of selecting the best now published in this book. As usual, special thanks go to **Simon Sharville** for his creative impact and diplomacy during the design process; **Sabine Reimer** for her usual effectiveness and healthy pragmatism during the production of Images 31 and **Stella Di Meo** who organised the exhibition with great care and developed a successful marketing and communications strategy.

We are also very grateful to **Andy Smith** who gave us his illustration 'A Lively Imagination' to create an eye-catching cover and to **Mark Taplin**, whose sketch for MTV's 'Sex, The Dirty Dozen' we used on the next call for entry form for Images 32.

Stuart Briers has again supported us with IT (and anything else) and demonstrated patience when faced with yet another question about the correct use of the AOI database. **Robert Lands**, Lawyer at Finers Stephens Innocent, has not only given us his expertise in legal matters but – after many years – is still interested in the well-being of our organisation.

Images 31 could not have been organised without the help of our dedicated casual staff and volunteers and we are very grateful for their invaluable assistance: **Chloe King**, **Faye Tabone**, **Nineta Avani**, **Naomi Manning**.

Last but not least, we are grateful for the support of the many organisations and individuals who contribute to the success of the Images exhibition and annual by submitting their work for others to judge.

The AOI Council and staff

Membership

The Association of Illustrators provides a voice for professional illustrators and by weight of numbers and expertise is able to enforce the rights of freelance illustrators at every stage of their careers.

Membership of the AOI is open to all professional illustrators, illustration students, agents, lecturers and illustration clients.

All categories of membership receive the following benefits:

- Free distribution of Varoom – the journal of illustration and made images, 90-page magazine celebrating the best in contemporary visual culture
- Free distribution of AOI info poster, UP! – *the* poster to hang on your wall!
- Discounted rates for Images – the best of contemporary British illustration
- Your contact details available on AOI database for enquiries from clients
- Discounts on art materials nationwide
- Large discounts on AOI events and publications

In addition we provide the following services for particular types of membership:

Full Membership
This category is for professional illustrators who have had a minimum of three works commissioned in the previous 12 months prior to application and accept the AOI code of conduct:

- Dedicated phone line for legal and pricing advice
- Substantial discount on portfolio surgeries with a professional consultant
- Business advice – an hour's free consultation with a chartered accountant on accounts, bookkeeping, National Insurance, VAT and tax
- Only full members are entitled to use the affix 'Mem AOI' and the AOI member logo on publicity
- Discounted Web promotion opportunities through AOI portfolios

Associate Membership
This allows the same benefits as full membership (without the prefix 'Mem AOI') but this category is designed to assist illustrators starting out in the industry or those who are returning to a career in illustration. Associate membership is reviewed regularly.

Student Membership
This service is for students on full-time illustration or related courses:
- Experts' advice on entering the profession
- Substantial discount on portfolio surgeries with a professional consultant
- Further discounts on AOI events, publications and competition entry
- Discounted Web promotion opportunities through AOI portfolios

Corporate Membership
This service is for agents and clients from the illustration industry who adhere to the AOI code of practice.
Further benefits:
- Free copy of the Images illustration annual
- All corporate members' staff and member agent represented illustrators will receive discounts on events, Images competition and AOI publications

College Membership
College membership entitles the college to the following benefits:
- Large discounts on AOI events and publications
- Link to college web page from AOI site
- Free copy of the Images illustration annual
- The right to use the AOI member logo on publicity
- Discounted Web promotion opportunities through AOI degree shows

Additional options (at extra cost) include:
- Portfolio consultations for groups or individual students
- Career Advice lecture covering self-promotion, copyright, pricing, licensing, the work of the AOI, and the speaker's working practice etc.
- Bulk publication orders of Survive – essential information for students on starting and/or Rights – covering aspects of the law likely to affect illustrators
- Degree show presence on AOI website – portfolio option to maximise your students exposure

For an application form and cost details please contact:
Association of Illustrators
2nd Floor, Back Building
150 Curtain Road
London EC2A 3AT

Tel: +44 (0) 20 7613 4328
Fax: +44 (0) 20 7613 4417

E-mail: info@theaoi.com
Website: www.theAOI.com

Publications

SURVIVE – The Illustrator's Guide to a Professional Career

Published by the AOI and last revised in 2001, Survive is the only comprehensive and in-depth guide to illustration as a professional career. Established illustrators, agents, clients and a range of other professionals have contributed to this fourth edition. Each area of the profession including portfolio presentation, self-promotion and copyright issues are looked at in detail. The wealth of information in Survive makes it absolutely indispensable to the newcomer and also has much to offer the more experienced illustrator.

RIGHTS - The Illustrator's Guide to Professional Practice

Rights is an all inclusive guide to aspects of the law specifically related to illustration. It includes information about copyright, contracts, book publishing agreements, agency agreements, how to seek legal advice, how to calculate fees and guidance on how to write a licence.
Rights is the result of a number of years research. It has been approved by solicitors and contains the most detailed and accurate model terms and conditions available for use by illustrators or clients.

REPORT ON ILLUSTRATION FEES AND STANDARDS OF PRICING

In 2005, the AOI have first published a report entitled 'Illustration Fees and Standards of Pricing'. The publication was revised in April 2007 with newest information from a recent online survey, new AOI data from the last two years and invaluable contributions from agents, art buyers and selected working professionals.
Properly researched costing and pricing structures is a central plank in maintaining business viability. Illustrators should consider the true cost of their services when determining rates. AOI hopes that this report will encourage both illustrators and commissioners to create awareness of the importance of carefully considered pricing.

CLIENT DIRECTORIES – now available online!

The Publishing Directory lists ca. 180 and the Editorial Directory more than 300 illustration clients with full contact details; the Advertising Directory holds details of over 200 advertising agencies who commission illustration – providing an invaluable source of information for all practitioners. Each directory includes notes of what kind of illustration is published by the client and we update and add contact details to each list every year.

VAROOM – the journal of illustration and made images

is a magazine devoted to exploring the world of illustration and image-making. It looks at practitioners from around the world who are making significant contributions to the ancient art of illustration, and provides writers, commentators and illustrators with a platform from which to take a critical look at trends and developments in the illustrated image.
Published three times a year. 90 pages, ISSN 1750-483X, available in specialist bookshops in the UK, Europe, USA and Canada, free to members.
www.varoom-mag.com

To order publications or subscribe to Varoom, please send a cheque, made payable to the Association of Illustrators, clearly stating your contact details and which publications you would like to purchase to:

AOI Publications
2nd Floor, Back Building
150 Curtain Road
London
EC2A 3AT

For payment by Visa, Mastercard or Maestro, please call +44 (0)20 7613 4328 or subscribe/order online: www.theAOI.com/publications

Information

UP! POSTER

Published quarterly, UP! is a collectible item each time featuring another unique image-maker. UP! not only looks good on your wall it also keeps you up to date with AOI news and events, reports on important industry developments and recommends exhibitions that could inspire you. UP! is designed by award winning design duo Non-Format, who also created the eye-catching look of Varoom.

DESPATCH Newsletter

Now published monthly, Despatch brings you the latest industry news, AOI events information, campaigns, initiatives and reviews of relevant exhibitions and publications. To subscribe, visit www.theaoi.com/submissions

www.theaoi.com - illustration resources for commissioners and practitioners

Visit the AOI's website for details of the Association's activities, including past and current Despatch newsletters and articles of our previous membership magazine, The Journal, details of forthcoming events and campaigns, the AOI's history, and to order publications, book tickets and display and browse online portfolios.

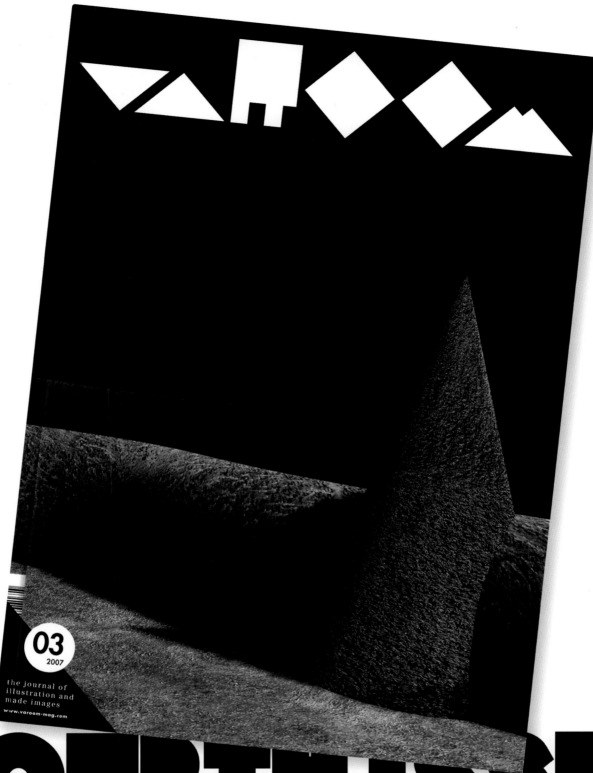

03
2007

the journal of
illustration and
made images

www.varoom-mag.com

FOURTH ISSUE OUT AUGUST 07